GRADE 4

envision®

An inspirational real-world program for gifted learners

By Melanie L. Bondy

Edited by Shanda Blue Easterday MFA, PhD

mind vine
P R E S S

Printed by: Data Reproductions Corporation
Auburn Hills, Michigan

DEDICATION

To my husband, Scott, and my son, Brendan, who have lovingly persevered with me and encouraged me in this process.

ACKNOWLEDGMENTS

For their support and encouragement: Richard and Marilyn Bondy, and Alvina Betka.

For being the most dedicated hard-working teachers I have ever had the pleasure of working with: Kristen Rabideau and Heidi Felstead.

To a dedicated teacher, Ginger Kern, who sought out quality challenge for her highest students, recognized the benefits of Envision, and encouraged me to continue my endeavors.

To my graphic artist, Michael Bartello, for his exceptional talent, kindness, and dedication.

To my editor, Shanda Blue Easterday, for her hard work, timeliness, and flexibility.

Copyright © 2008 Melanie L. Bondy

Bondy, Melanie L.

Envision, Grade 4: Melanie L. Bondy: edited by Shanda Blue Easterday, MFA, PhD.

Cover and book design by Michael Bartello, www.seesponge.com.

Printed in the United States of America.

Referenced with permission: *Taxonomy of Educational Objectives: Book 1: Cognitive Domain*, Benjamin S. Bloom, Ed. Copyright © 1956, 1984. Pearson Allyn and Bacon, Boston, MA.

Mind Vine Press, LLC
70727 Copper Boulevard
Lawton, MI 49065

mindvinepress.com

ISBN: 978-0-9786715-6-3

TABLE OF CONTENTS

AUTHOR LETTER:
A SOLUTION TO TEACHING
GIFTED STUDENTS

A SOLUTION TO TEACHING GIFTED STUDENTS

Teaching has always meant more than presenting lessons, assigning homework, and grading papers. Today, educators are asked to micromanage a host of objectives and topics that stretch far beyond the standard core curriculum. While tackling these new responsibilities, teachers must still contend with the challenge of educating an often under-served population of students: the gifted, whose needs are substantially different from those of most of their classmates.

As a teacher, I struggled to provide the best education I could for all my students. In my first class of thirty-five students I had five students who were in a cluster group for the gifted. I worked long hours to find and create innovative lessons for the thirty non-gifted students, and then endeavored to adapt each lesson to accommodate my five cluster students.

I was fortunate, in that first year of teaching, to take part in a one-year training program for teaching the gifted, and I learned of the available strategies for teaching gifted students. I looked forward to these strategies helping my gifted students excel in school, and I became motivated and energized to utilize them right away.

As I began implementing the techniques I had learned, which included supplying research projects, explorations, logic exercises, and high-level thinking games, I believed these new exercises were sufficiently challenging my gifted students. After only about a week with each new activity, however, I noticed that they were becoming repetitive and mundane. The logic problems offered different scenarios, but all employed the same type of thinking. Once the students understood the first few problems, solving the rest became mechanical. In addition, the problems had little or no relationship to the students' personal lives.

The research projects and explorations I had so hopefully adopted proved, in a classroom setting, to be haphazardly grouped, difficult to manage, extremely broad and unclear in their requirements, and too subject-specific to allow for much curriculum flexibility. They were also not in-depth enough to engage the students for more than a few weeks.

Of additional significance, I found that I had no valuable way of assessing—and therefore promoting—student advancement. The logic exercises, for example, included answer keys, but the keys offered no means to evaluate the levels of thinking associated with solving the problems. Answers were simply right or wrong. Similarly, the thinking games, explorations, and research projects all defied useful assessment, leaving me to guess at where my students were and where they were poised to go. A colorful portfolio showcasing the end products of various broad activities and repetitive projects is a poor substitute for a thorough, convincing record of demonstrable advancement in high-level thinking.

Although the gifted students were enjoying their new extra activities, they were, in fact, being little more than entertained. At this point, though frustrated from researching and prepping materials that had proved to be of such limited value, I was unwilling to accept that "the best available" was the best I could offer my gifted students. I grew more determined than ever to find a solution to this nagging problem.

To solve the problem, I developed Envision, a gifted program that is exciting and challenging, that leads students through the highest levels of thinking, and that appeals to diverse interests by having deep roots in the real world. Because Envision draws on all subject areas, students can work on their projects at any time of the day, during any class period, and still be connected to the general work of the class. Envision includes a climactic succession of related projects with concrete objectives.

Of special importance to me is that each student's progress is subject to clear, consistent, unambiguous assessment at predetermined stages from start to finish. Also, the program is ambitious enough in its depth and scope to engage, challenge, and reward gifted students all year long. Finally, Envision is a program that gifted students work on with minimal oversight, which encourages independent learning and, as a practical concern, allows more time for the teacher to address other classroom needs.

PROGRAM INTRODUCTION:
THE ENVISION EXPERIENCE

THE ENVISION EXPERIENCE

What is Envision?

Envision is a real-world independent study program for gifted and talented students who are not sufficiently challenged by the standard curriculum. It includes a series of four multidisciplinary projects, one for each school quarter, and is designed to span the entire school year.

What type of class can use Envision?

Intended to complement or replace the standard curriculum, the projects integrate advanced academic study with real-world experience and problem solving. Since the projects are not subject-specific, drawing as they do from all disciplines, they can be integrated easily into any type of classroom curriculum. The Envision program is also flexible enough to be used in a regular education classroom that has gifted and talented students or in a classroom of only gifted students.

Which students can participate in Envision?

Students who participate in the program are those who are identified, based on school or district criteria, as being gifted, talented, or advanced learners.

IMPORTANT!

Almost positively, especially after seeing the first projects completed, your non-gifted students will want to participate in the Envision program. Allowing these students to participate in Envision will not only excite and motivate them even more about school, but will also make you feel good knowing that you are providing the best opportunities for all of your students. Even non-gifted students can take on the Envision challenges and will probably surprise you with their level of enthusiasm and learning.

Allowing non-gifted students to participate may require some extra work on your part. For instance, you may choose to modify the Student Instruction Guides, you may have more photocopying to do, and you may need to hold a larger Project Expo. However, expanding participation to more students will greatly reward both you and them.

Can the projects be implemented in any order?

While any one project can be taught independently from the other three, the program is most effective when all four are undertaken in chronological order and as a series. The order in which the projects are implemented is determined after considering the levels of Benjamin S. Bloom's Taxonomy of Educational Objectives (Bloom, 1956, 1984) contained in each project, the complexity of each project's topic, and the amount of work required for each project.

The first project in the series is designed to familiarize students with a new style of learning, and, for that reason, has a lighter topic. The second and third projects' topics are more complex in their subject matter, which adds an extra dimension of challenge for experienced Envision learners. The fourth and final project is designed with the end of the school year in mind. Its topic is lighter, yet the objectives continue to challenge students in new, creative ways. There are detailed descriptions of the projects in the last section of this introduction.

THE ENVISION EXPERIENCE

How are the student materials organized?

At the beginning of the quarter, Envision students receive a Student Instruction Guide containing all the instruction needed for the upcoming project. The instruction guide allows students to work on their projects independently, guiding them step-by-step through the project.

If students need additional guidance along the way, a set of important Student Resource Cards is included and offers a wide range of supplemental instruction. The resource cards offer definitions, helpful tips, and visual examples for certain tasks listed on the Student Instruction Guide.

Though the teacher introduces the program and is available for periodic guidance, encouragement, and assessment, the Student Instruction Guide and the resource cards enable students to work largely on their own and at their own pace. This structure encourages independent learning on the part of the Envision student, while allowing the teacher ample time to attend to his or her regular responsibilities.

At the completion of each project, students receive a Student Self-Assessment, which gives them the opportunity to reflect on and assess their own work.

How are the teacher materials organized?

Following this introduction, you will find a Teacher Instruction Guide. The Teacher Instruction Guide is presented in a step-by-step format and explains project implementation from start to finish. It includes detailed instructions, examples, and references to all the forms and materials you will use along the way.

In addition to the Teacher Instruction Guide are four Project Appendices. The appendices contain all the letters, charts, invitations, signs, certificates, and assessments needed to complete the Envision program. These reproducible forms are grouped by project and are provided in order of use.

What additional materials does the program include?

The entire Envision program package is thorough and complete. In addition to this manual, the package contains all additional supplemental materials needed to integrate Envision smoothly into any classroom. The materials include Project Expo Posters, a Bulletin Board Banner, the Student Resource Cards previously discussed, and a specially designed CD. The CD contains all the PDF files of forms, in color and with typeable fields. There is also useful information for both teachers and students at mindvinepress.com.

What is Bloom's Taxonomy of Educational Objectives?

Benjamin S. Bloom's Taxonomy of Educational Objectives is a model that presents thinking as occurring at six levels, and ranks those levels from the least complex, or lowest level, to the most abstract, or highest level. The type of cognition that occurs at any given level distinguishes that level from the others. At the lower end, in Bloom's original 1956 Taxonomy, are Knowledge, Comprehension, and Application, in rising order. At the higher end are Analysis, Synthesis, and, ultimately, Evaluation.

Over the decades, however, educators who have worked with Bloom's Taxonomy have made a significant change to the hierarchy of cognitive activities. In most educational circles, Synthesis now ranks above Evaluation as the highest level, making Evaluation the second highest.

What distinguishes each of the Bloom's levels?

A practical way to understand these six levels of thinking and how they relate to one another is to know the cognitive activity that occurs at each level, and the skills associated with each cognitive activity.

Knowledge, at the lowest cognitive level, involves recalling something previously encountered, but does not involve understanding or applying that knowledge. Related skills include memorizing, listing, defining, quoting, naming, simple labeling, locating, and knowing who, when, where, what, and how many.

Comprehension requires that a student understand knowledge, such as the nature of an important event, for example, rather than merely when and where the event occurred. Comprehension does not, however, require the student to apply that knowledge to other knowledge, such as a similar event. Related skills include summarizing, describing, estimating, interpreting, outlining, collecting, demonstrating, and understanding how as opposed to simply how many.

Application happens when a student uses learned knowledge to solve new problems in new situations. Related skills include calculating, solving, experimenting, resolving, and answering.

Analysis, the first of the three highest-level activities, occurs when a student dissects a concept or object into its component parts and examines those parts separately and in relation to one another or to the whole. Related skills include separating, ordering, diagramming, classifying, dividing, comparing, contrasting, and finding patterns.

Evaluation means offering an opinion on the value of information, events, or concepts based on specific criteria. Related skills include assessing, ranking, persuading, judging, supporting, and refuting.

Synthesis, widely considered the most abstract kind of thinking, occurs when a student can restructure the parts of a whole into something new. The ability to create something new from what has been learned requires a thorough understanding of the subject matter, an understanding of its applications and its parts, and an evaluative opinion regarding each part's importance and relevance to the whole. Related skills include integrating, revising, rearranging, substituting, designing, composing, building, organizing, interviewing, hypothesizing, and inventing.

IMPORTANT!

The levels described above are cumulative. For example, the highest level of thinking, Synthesis, incorporates all other levels of thinking: Knowledge, Comprehension, Application, Analysis, and Evaluation. Please keep this in mind when reviewing each Envision project's connection to Bloom's Taxonomy discussed below.

What is Envision's connection to Bloom's Taxonomy?

As mentioned above, each project teaches a specific, varied set of advanced objectives that have been carefully selected and organized according to Benjamin S. Bloom's widely accepted and updated Taxonomy of Educational Objectives. Although the projects incorporate all levels of thinking, the bulk of the objectives for each project focuses on exercising the three highest levels.

If you would like to see each project's connection to the Bloom's Taxonomy levels, go to the beginning of each project appendix:

- Appendix 1: "Backyard Getaway and Bloom's Taxonomy"
- Appendix 2: "Environmental Declaration and Bloom's Taxonomy"
- Appendix 3: "Civic Mission and Bloom's Taxonomy"
- Appendix 4: "Fitness Pursuit and Bloom's Taxonomy"

What are the four Envision projects?

For each Envision project, students are guided to create a comprehensive portfolio, a formal classroom presentation, and an exhibit presented at an Envision project expo.

Backyard Getaway (Project 1): As the first project in the series, Backyard Getaway immediately engages students in the Envision program by being as much fun as it is educational. Students are challenged to design a complete personalized dream backyard using one acre of land.

Students will research and make decisions in order to create and develop five specific areas within their Backyard Getaways: a relaxation area, a recreation area, a water habitat, a flower or food garden, and a state or country tribute area. Each student will create a data table, maps, a personal reflection, safety signs, a watercolor, a food chain, a poem, a t-chart, and a fictional story. All of these written materials will be collected in a portfolio.

Each student will then design and create an exhibit that captures and conveys the highlights of his or her backyard. The exhibit will include a relaxation area diorama, a flower or food garden flipbook, a state or country miniature museum, and a backyard model. Students will also present their project to the class and participate in the project expo.

Environmental Declaration (Project 2): The second Envision project is designed to create a deep awareness about a state or national environmental issue and to allow students a voice in the matter. Each student will have the opportunity to research environmental issues and choose a specific issue on which to focus. In the project portfolio, each student will create a crossword puzzle, a line graph, an actions card, a mailing list, a persuasive letter, a bumper sticker, and an illustration.

The project exhibit will showcase the portfolio and be visually informative by displaying a picture cube geared toward core democratic values, a "do's and don'ts" poster, and visual examples of environmental affects or solutions. Each student will also make a documentary about his or her issue and share it for the classroom presentation and at the expo.

THE ENVISION EXPERIENCE

Civic Mission (Project 3): The third Envision project allows students to interact and learn within their community while performing a service. Students have the rewarding experience of evaluating personal interests and talents, creating an academic goal, and forming a partnership with a locality of their choice.

Each student will have the opportunity to work with a community member to discuss the locality's needs and possible solutions. In the portfolio, students will create a service action plan based on solving one or more of the locality's needs, a journal, a post-event personal reflection, and a creative thank-you card.

At their project exhibit students will share their portfolios, t-shirt designs, and mobiles of learning. As part of an in-class presentation and the concluding project expo, each student will teach one aspect of an academic goal learned during the process, share a personal challenge that was overcome, and conclude with positive message to inspire others to participate in service learning.

Fitness Pursuit (Project 4): The final project of the year energizes students with the opportunity to develop an in-depth plan of healthy habits by which to live.

Students will focus on four main areas of personal health: sleep health, healthy eating, physical health, and a healthy brain. Each student will create a personal sleep log, double-line graph, healthy eating investigation, personal food pyramid, healthy eating regimen, sentence scramble, exercise duration clocks, safety test, homework schedule, and match-up illustration.

For the project exhibit, each student will create a room art piece, an academic activities list, and a one-month master calendar.

With the Envision program, you will be confident that your gifted students are continually being fully challenged at high levels while being enriched with the freedoms of choice and creative expression. Envision will inspire their educational experiences on a daily basis. Your gifted students will look forward to each new Envision learning endeavor and, most importantly, to their own futures.

TEACHER INSTRUCTION GUIDE FOR PROJECT IMPLEMENTATION

TEACHER INSTRUCTION GUIDE

You are now ready to begin implementing the Envision program in your classroom. This Teacher Instruction Guide serves as a comprehensive checklist for every step necessary to achieve success. The instruction guide is based on a school year comprised of four ten-week quarters, but can be modified to suit your needs.

> **IMPORTANT!**
> Since the project format for each ten-week term is the same, you will use this instruction guide for implementing each of the four Envision projects.

 Every step in the Teacher Instruction Guide includes detailed instructions and visual examples. Because you will start with the Backyard Getaway Project, the examples included in this guide are based on Backyard Getaway.

STEP 1
Planning and Preparing for the Quarter

The first form, the Teacher Planning Guide, allows you to plan every stage of each project from start to finish. Setting dates and times for project events well in advance will guarantee the best possible outcome.

Students should be given an entire quarter or about ten weeks to work on and complete each project. This ten-week period can be slightly flexible, give or take a week, as needed.

Note: The Teacher Instruction Guide walks you through the entire project implementation process. Forms you will use are included with each step in the order they are needed. It is best to do the photocopying as you proceed with each step, rather than copying everything up front, since many forms will need to be filled in prior to photocopying. Located in each project Appendix is a Teacher Copy Chart that lists each form you will need, when you will need it, and how many copies you will need.

1.1 Copy one Teacher Planning Guide.

1.2 Use the guidelines below, along with the chart that follows, to guide you in filling out your personal Teacher Planning Guide. It may be helpful to start with Week 10 and work in reverse.

Week 1 Preparation, Introduction, Implementation:
- 30 minutes outside of class for initial planning and preparing (Steps 1.1-1.2).
- 15 minutes outside of class to prepare for Project Introduction (2.1-2.3).
- 20 minutes of class time for Project Introduction (2.4-2.7). The Project Introduction should be presented at least one day prior to Project Implementation (below).
- 20 minutes outside of class to prepare for Project Implementation (3.1-3.6).
- 30 minutes of class time for Project Implementation (3.7-3.17).

Weeks 2, 4, and 6: No teacher preparation or scheduled events. Students continue to work on their projects during these weeks.

Weeks 3, 5, 7 Checkpoint Meetings:
- 10 minutes outside of class to prepare for the Checkpoint Meetings (4.1-4.2).
- 10 minutes of class time to distribute Checkpoint Organizers (4.3-4.6). Distribute the Checkpoint Organizers two to three days prior to the Checkpoint Meetings (below).
- 10 minutes of class time, per every five to six Envision students, to conduct Checkpoint Meetings (4.7-4.12).

Week 8 Preparation, Invitations:
- 10 minutes outside of class to prepare for the Project Expo (5.1-5.2).
- 10 minutes of class time to Invite Families to the Project Expo (5.3-5.4).
- 60 minutes outside of class to continue preparation for the Project Expo (5.5-5.11).

Week 9 Preparation, Classroom Presentations, Classroom Expo, Student Self-Assessment:
- 30 minutes outside of class, plus an optional store trip, to prepare for the Classroom Presentations and Project Expo (5.12-5.15). Prepare two to three days prior to Classroom Presentations (below).
- 5 minutes of class time, per Envision student, to conduct the Classroom Presentations (6A.1-6A.13 or 6B.1-6B.12). The Classroom Presentations should be on the same day and during the same time block as the Classroom Expo and Student Self-Assessment (below).
- 5 minutes of class time, per each Envision student, plus an additional 10 minutes for the Classroom Expo and Student Self-Assessment (7A.1-7A.9 or 7B.1-7B.10).

Week 10 Final Preparation, Project Expo, Teacher Assessment:
- 45 minutes outside of class to complete Final Preparation for the Project Expo (8.1-8.10). This preparation will need to be done on the day of the Project Expo.
- 60 minutes of class time to conduct the Project Expo (9.1-9.4). Scheduling the expo in the evening ensures better attendance by parents.
- 2 store trips plus 10 minutes outside of class per each Envision student, for the Conclusion and Teacher Assessment (10.1-10.8).
- 15 minutes of class time for Student Review (10.9-10.10).

TEACHER PLANING GUIDE

Events scheduled with the class are in black.

Week	Event (Step Numbers)	Time Required
1	Planning and Preparing for the Quarter (1.1-1.2)	30 min.
	Prepare for Project Introduction (2.1-2.3)	15 min.
	Project Introduction (2.4-2.7) (prior day to Project Implementation)	20 min.
	Preparation for Project Implementation (3.1-3.6)	20 min.
	Project Implementation (3.7-3.17)	30 min.
2	No teacher preparation during this week. Students continue to work on their projects.	
3	Preparation for the Checkpoint Meetings (4.1-4.2)	10 min.
	Distribute Checkpoint Organizers (4.3-4.6) 2-3 days prior to Meetings	10 min.
	Checkpoint Meetings (4.7-4.12) (For every 5-6 Envision students)	10 min.
4	No teacher preparation during this week. Students continue to work on their projects.	
5	Preparation for the Checkpoint Meetings (4.1-4.2)	10 min.
	Distribute Checkpoint Organizers (4.3-4.6) 2-3 days prior to Meetings	10 min.
	Checkpoint Meetings (4.7-4.12) (For every 5-6 Envision students)	10 min.
6	No teacher preparation during this week. Students continue to work on their projects.	
7	Preparation for the Checkpoint Meetings (4.1-4.2)	10 min.
	Distribute Checkpoint Organizers (4.3-4.6) 2-3 days prior to Meetings	10 min.
	Checkpoint Meetings (4.7-4.12) (For every 5-6 Envision students)	10 min.
8	Preparation for the Project Expo (5.1-5.2)	10 min.
	Invite Families to the Project Expo (5.3-5.4)	10 min.
	Preparation for the Project Expo Ctd. (5.5-5.11)	60 min.
9	Preparation for Classroom Presentations and the Project Expo (5.12-5.15) 2-3 days prior to Presentations	30 min. (+ store: optional)
	Classroom Presentations (6A.1-6A.13 or 6B.1-6B.12) Same time-block as Classroom Expo and Student Self-Assessment	5 min. per Envision student
	Classroom Expo and Student Self-Assessment (7A.1-7A.9 or 7B.1-7B.10)	5 min. per Envision student + 10 min.
10	Final Preparation for the Project Expo (8.1-8.10) the day of the Expo	45 min.
	Project Expo (9.1-9.4) preferably in evening to ensure parent availability	60 min.
	Conclusion and Teacher Assessment (10.1-10.8)	2 trips to store +10 min./student
	Student Review (10.9-10.10)	15 min.

TEACHER INSTRUCTION GUIDE

STEP 2
Student Introduction

> **IMPORTANT!**
> If you would like to see each project's specific connections to the Bloom's Taxonomy levels, you will find a document at the beginning of each Project Appendix:
> - Appendix 1: Backyard Getaway and Bloom's Taxonomy
> - Appendix 2: Environmental Declaration and Bloom's Taxonomy
> - Appendix 3: Civic Mission and Bloom's Taxonomy
> - Appendix 4: Fitness Pursuit and Bloom's Taxonomy

Prepare for Project Introduction:

2.1 Make a copy of one Parent Envision Introduction Letter (for Backyard Getaway project only), one Parent Project Introduction Letter, one Student Project Introduction Letter, and one Student Instruction Guide.

2.2 Using the information from your Teacher Planning Guide, complete the Parent Envision Introduction Letter (Backyard Getaway only), Parent Project Introduction Letter, and Student Project Introduction Letter.

> **IMPORTANT!**
> When completing the information on the forms, remember that there are two options:
> 1. You may choose to photocopy the form from the corresponding appendix and fill in the blanks by hand.
>
> **OR**
>
> 2. You may use the CD to type in the blanks, then print the form in color or black and white.

2.3 Copy a completed Parent Envision Introduction Letter (Backyard Getaway only), and a Parent Project Introduction Letter for each student. Do not make multiple copies of the Student Introduction Letter or Student Instruction Guide at this time. You will need only one of each of these right now.

Project Introduction:

2.4 Bring your gifted students together and, referring to the Parent Envision Introduction Letter, give them an overview of the Envision Program.

2.5 Read aloud the Student Introduction Letter to give students an overview of the project. Refer to the Student Instruction Guide to highlight some of the project tasks.

2.6 Backyard Getaway Only: To each student, hand out one Parent Envision Introduction Letter to take home. Explain that the bottom portion of it contains an Envision Permission Form that the parent should sign, detach, and return to you as soon as possible.

2.7 To each student, hand out one Parent Project Introduction Letter to take home.

 introduction letter

Dear Parent(s),

I am happy to inform you that your child has been invited to participate in an advanced academic program called Envision. I am sending you this letter to explain the program and ask for your permission to include your child in this special opportunity.

Envision is an exciting, yearlong program designed for students who are not sufficiently challenged by the standard grade-level curriculum. The focus of the program is on developing high-level critical thinking and creativity, and encourages students to *envision* how they might achieve their goals for the future. Envision guides students through four real-world-based projects, one for each quarter of the school year.

In chronological order, the four projects are: Backyard Getaway, Environmental Declaration, Civic Mission, and Fitness Pursuit. Backyard Getaway allows students to design a complete, personalized dream backyard using one acre of land. Environmental Declaration is designed to create a deep awareness about a state or national environmental issue and allow students a voice in the matter. The third project, Civic Mission, allows students to interact and learn within their community while performing a service. Finally, Fitness Pursuit energizes students with the opportunity to cultivate an in-depth awareness of healthy habits to live by. Each project introduces new ideas, new vocabulary, new technology, and new challenges.

Students will work on Envision during class time, free time, and at home.

To give permission for your child to participate in Envision, simply sign the Envision Permission Form at the bottom of this letter, detach it, and return the form to me. If you want your child to participate in Envision, please read the attached Parent Backyard Getaway Introduction Letter. The letter introduces you to the first project, informs you of important dates, and requests permission for your child's continued participation. You will receive a Parent Project Introduction Letter at the beginning of each quarter with the start of each new project.

Envision promises to be a wonderful learning opportunity for your child. I look forward to hearing from you. Please feel free to contact me if you have any questions.

Sincerely,

Mrs. Bondy

269-978-7227 · bondyme@school.org

- -

permission form

Please fill out this section, detach, and return as soon as possible.   Date: *September 6, 2XXX*

❑ I have read the Parent Envision Introduction Letter and give my child permission to participate in the Envision program.

❑ I have read the Parent Envision Introduction Letter and do not give my child permission to participate in the Envision program.

Child's Name: *Alyssa Good*   Parent's Signature: *Joanne Good*

BACKYARD GETAWAY

parent backyard getaway introduction letter

Dear Parent(s),

Welcome to Backyard Getaway, the first of four Envision projects that will challenge and inspire your child. Backyard Getaway will immediately engage your child as its challenge is to design a complete, personalized dream backyard using one acre of land.

For this project, your child will research and make decisions in order to create and develop five specific areas within his or her backyard: a relaxation area, a recreation area, a water habitat, a flower or food garden, and a state or country tribute area. Your child will create a table, maps, a personal reflection, safety signs, a watercolor, a food chain, a poem, a t-chart, and a fictional story. All of these written materials will be collected in a portfolio. Next, your child will build an exhibit including a display board, diorama, flipbook, miniature museum, backyard model, and finishing touches that highlight key aspects of the backyard. Lastly, your child will give a brief formal presentation to the class.

A Student Instruction Guide will be provided to guide your child, step by step, through this process. The Instruction Guide is a comprehensive list of project requirements and is designed to engage higher-level thinking. The guide also references helpful Resource Cards, which provide additional explanations, ideas, tips, and directions. There will be a set of these cards in our classroom to which your child can refer.

Backyard Getaway is designed to be worked on independently during class time, free time, and at home. By scheduling several Checkpoint Meeting dates throughout the quarter, I will be able to monitor each student's progress. On these dates, I will meet with each student to discuss accomplishments and plan goals for the next checkpoint. I will also address any difficulties students might be having.

Backyard Getaway will conclude with a Project Expo. The expo will be your child's opportunity to share his or her finished project with family, friends, and other guests. You will receive a detailed invitation to the Project Expo later in the quarter.

Dates to Remember:

Checkpoint 1: *September 18, 2XXX*

Checkpoint 2: *October 2, 2XXX*

Checkpoint 3: *October 16, 2XXX*

Classroom Presentation: *November 1, 2XXX*

Backyard Getaway Expo: *November 7, 2XXX 6:30 - 7:30 pm*

Sincerely,

Mrs. Bondy

269-978-7227 · bondyme@school.org

BACKYARD GETAWAY

student backyard getaway introduction letter

Dear Student,

Welcome to Backyard Getaway! This is the first of four projects you will embark on as part of the Envision Program experience. Backyard Getaway is about creating a paradise escape or a place you can get away to whenever you like. It is also a journey of discovery, research, and creativity.

The project begins with your receiving an imaginary plot of land measuring one acre in size. Keeping this size in mind, you will create five unique areas within your backyard: a relaxation area, a recreation area, a water habitat, a flower or food garden, and a state or country tribute area. For this project, you have no budget; the sky is the limit!

Backyard Getaway contains four components. The first will be to conduct research and create numerous components for your backyard areas. You will organize this information in a project portfolio. The second will be to create an exhibit that displays additional backyard components you will create. The third will be to share your completed portfolio and exhibit with your classmates. To do this you will give a brief formal presentation. During your presentation you will explain key aspects of your Backyard Getaway. Last will be the Project Expo, an event that celebrates your hard work and achievements. This final component allows you the opportunity to invite family and friends to share in your success.

You will work on Backyard Getaway throughout the school day, during your free time, and at home. Generally, you will be expected to work on your own. You will consult with me periodically at Checkpoint Meetings to discuss your progress and receive guidance. Between the checkpoints, feel free to discuss your project with other Envision students.

The attached Student Instruction Guide contains all the information you will need to complete the required Backyard Getaway Project successfully. The Instruction Guide will challenge you to be resourceful, organized, and to think at a higher level.

Dates to Remember:

Checkpoint 1: *September 18, 2XXX*

Checkpoint 2: *October 2, 2XXX*

Checkpoint 3: *October 16, 2XXX*

Classroom Presentation: *November 1, 2XXX*

Backyard Getaway Expo: *November 7, 2XXX 6:30 - 7:30 pm*

After reading this introduction, you are now ready to begin thinking about your Backyard Getaway. Good luck and have fun!

Sincerely,

Mrs. Bondy

269-978-7227 · bondyme@school.org

STUDENT INSTRUCTION GUIDE

Building Your Project Portfolio • Creating Your Project Exhibit
Presenting Your Project • Attending the Expo

CREATIVITY IS HIGHLY ENCOURAGED!

IMPORTANT!

Available resource cards are denoted by a Backyard Getaway icon . When you see one of these icons, you will know that there is a corresponding resource card available that gives additional helpful information and depicts visual examples for your reference. Also be sure to visit www. mindvinepress.com, other trustworthy Internet sites, and library reference materials for additional resources and examples.

COMPONENT 1

Building Your Project Portfolio Total Possible Portfolio Points: 79 out of 100 total possible for project

Get ready! It is now time to plan and make decisions about the backyard of your dreams. This will be a wonderful experience and opportunity to engage your intellectual abilities as well as your imagination. Complete the numbered requirements below, in order, as they build upon one another and will guide you smoothly through the process. Good luck!

Note: "Component 1: Building Your Backyard Getaway Portfolio" is separated into two sections: "Portfolio Section 1: Climate and Terrain Features" and "Portfolio Section 2: Area Locations".

STEP 3
Project Implementation

Prepare for Project Implementation:

The Student Commitment Contract mentioned below ensures that students and their parents understand and are accountable for project work time and Checkpoint Meeting expectations. It creates a formal commitment to these expectations and an understanding that students could lose their Envision privileges if they do not follow them. It also reminds students and parents of important project dates.

3.1 Copy one Teacher Forms Checklist and one Student Commitment Contract.

3.2 Fill in the Envision student names on the Teacher Forms Checklist and set it aside for later use.

3.3 Using the event dates from your Teacher Planning Guide, complete the Student Commitment Contract.

3.4 Make a copy of the completed Student Commitment Contract for each Envision student.

3.5 Copy a completed Student Project Introduction Letter and Student Instruction Guide, both previously used in Step 2, for each of your gifted students. Staple the Student Project Introduction Letter and guide together as a packet, placing the introduction letter on top.

Note: You may also want to copy the smaller sized resource card pages in the corresponding Project Appendix to include with each student letter and guide. This is not necessary, since there is the classroom set of resource cards, but may be helpful to students when they work on Envision outside of the classroom.

3.6 Decide on a specific location to keep the Project Resource Cards. Take out and set aside the set of cards for the project you are implementing.

TEACHER INSTRUCTION GUIDE

Project Implementation:

3.7 Use your Teacher Forms Checklist (Step 3.1) to record each signed Envision Permission Form (distributed in Step 2.6) that is returned to you.

3.8 Distribute a Student Commitment Contract (Step 3.4) to each of your Envision students.

3.9 Review the contract with your students and answer any questions they have.

3.10 Ask each student to sign the contract, thereby agreeing to its expectations.

3.11 Direct students to take their Student Commitment Contracts home to be signed by a parent and returned to you as soon as possible.

3.12 Distribute a student packet (Step 3.5) to each of your contracted Envision students.

3.13 Read the Student Introduction Letter and review the remainder of the student packet materials together.

3.14 Share two to three resource cards with the students and explain how they correspond to particular requirements on the Student Instruction Guide. Show students where the resource cards will be kept.

IMPORTANT!

Stress to students that the Student Instruction Guide gives only the essentials for the tasks, allowing for student creativity. However, the resource cards are available to lend additional support by supplying definitions, explanations, tips, and visual examples.

3.15 Direct students to keep their materials in a safe, handy place. Let them know that they can now work on the project at school, during extra time, and at home. Tell them it is their responsibility to bring their project materials back and forth each day.

3.16 Allow students to begin using available class time to work on Envision.

3.17 Record the receipt of the signed Student Commitment Contracts on the Teacher Forms Checklist as they are returned.

TEACHER FORMS CHECKLIST

use this checklist to record forms submitted by the students

student name	envision permission form	student commitment contract	student checkpoint organizer 1	student checkpoint organizer 2	student checkpoint organizer 3	expo invitation response number attending special equip.needed
1. Michael	✓					
2. Alysssa	✓					
3. Brian	✓					
4. Alex	✓					
5. Lauren	✓					
6. Brendan	✓					
7. Ella	✓					
8. Teagan	✓					
9. Earl	✓					
10.						
11.						
12.						
13.						
14.						
15.						
16.						
17.						
18.						
19.						
20.						
21.						
22.						
23.						
24.						
25.						

STUDENT COMMITMENT CONTRACT

expectations

project work time

I agree to:

- be responsible for following my Student Instruction Guide to do my work.
- keep track of all my project materials.
- work hard on Envision without disturbing others.
- save my unanswered questions until my teacher is free to talk.

checkpoint meetings

I will come prepared with:

- my Student Instruction Guide.
- my completed Student Checkpoint Organizer.
- all of my project materials.

important dates and times

Checkpoint 1: *September 18, 2XXX*

Checkpoint 2: *October 2, 2XXX*

Checkpoint 3: *October 16, 2XXX*

Classroom Presentation: *November 1, 2XXX*

Backyard Getaway Expo: *November 7, 2XXX*
6:30 - 7:30 pm

signatures

I agree to:

- meet expectations on the dates listed above.
- complete each of the Backyard Getaway requirements to the best of my ability.
- bring my project work to school each day so that I can work on it during extra time.
- take my project work from school each night so that I can work on it at home.

I understand that the Envision Backyard Getaway Project is a special opportunity, and that if I do not meet the above expectations, I may be asked to return to normal classroom activities.

Student Signature: *Alyssa Good*   Date: *September 6, 2XXX*

Parent Signature: *Joanne Good*   Date: *September 6, 2XXX*

Please return this contract by: *September 7, 2XXX*

PHYSICAL MAP

RELAXATION AREA DIORAMA

ROAD MAP

EXAMPLE

A road map does not always show only roads. It can also show various points of interest in an area. Your backyard road map will be created as you progress through Component 2 of your Student Instruction Guide. Keep your map consistent with the way you created your physical map with regards to media and style so that it is easy to create and read.

Begin with an outline of your physical map. Draw and label the area locations in your backyard as you work on the Area Location objectives. Create a key with symbols if needed. Be sure to include your creative map title and map scale.

Michael's Restful Retreat Road Map

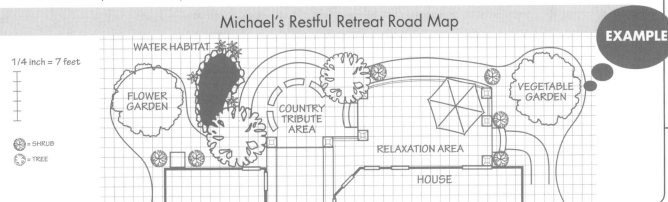

STEP 4
Checkpoint Meetings

Although Envision is an independent study program, your interaction and guidance are crucial to each student's success. The checkpoint process assures students that they will have a scheduled time to receive your personal attention. It also allows them to share their accomplishments to date and ask any questions they may have. At each Checkpoint Meeting, you can assess progress and lend support and direction, encouraging the students to stay on track to meet upcoming deadlines. To help schedule and run your checkpoints smoothly, complete the following steps.

IMPORTANT!

You will revisit this section (Step 4) each time you plan to conduct a Checkpoint Meeting.

Preparation for Checkpoint Meetings:

4.1 Copy a Student Checkpoint Organizer for each of your Envision students.

4.2 Copy one Teacher Checkpoint Record and fill in your Envision student names.

Distribute Checkpoint Organizers:

4.3 Distribute the Student Checkpoint Organizers to your Envision students. Have each student fill in his or her name, the upcoming Checkpoint Date, and his or her climate choice.

4.4 Explain to the students that in a few days you will be meeting with them to discuss their projects. Explain that they will each need to complete the Student Checkpoint Organizer and bring it on that day.

4.5 Read through the organizer with them and answer any questions.

4.6 Direct the students to complete their organizer over the next few days and bring it to the Checkpoint Meeting.

Checkpoint Meetings:

4.7 While your non-Envision students are working, ask a group of five to six Envision students to meet with you for a Checkpoint Meeting. Remind them to bring their completed Student Checkpoint Organizers, Student Instruction Guides, and project materials.

4.8 Using the Student Checkpoint Organizers, allow each student to respond to each question. Ask students to expand on their answers when necessary. Offer assistance where needed.

4.9 Use your Teacher Checkpoint Record to record any notes you wish to make.

4.10 Conclude the meeting by collecting the Student Checkpoint Organizers to keep for your records.

4.11 Keep your Teacher Checkpoint Record for use at all Checkpoint Meetings and for your records.

4.12 Direct the first group of students to return to their seats and ask your next group of five to six Envision students to meet with you for a Checkpoint Meeting.

Repeat Steps 4.7 through 4.12 until all your Envision students have had a meeting.

STUDENT CHECKPOINT ORGANIZER

EXAMPLE

Student Name: *Brendan*   Checkpoint Date: *September 18, 2XXX*

Climate Choice: *Average temperatures: 18-75° F, Average precipitation: 23-30"*

directions

1. Using your Student Instruction Guide check off any requirements that you have completed up to this point.

2. Bring the following items to the Checkpoint Meeting:

• your Student Instruction Guide.

• your completed Student Checkpoint Organizer.

• all of your project materials.

questions

1. Which requirements have you completed up to this point?

All of Portfolio Section 1 and the relaxation area reflection. It was all fun!

2. Is there anything you need help with?

I'd like help getting a box for my diorama.

3. Is there anything else about your project that you would like to discuss?

Will you look over my relaxation area reflection?

4. List at least three goals you expect to accomplish by the next checkpoint.

I plan to finish my relaxation area and water habitat objectives by the next checkpoint.

TEACHER CHECKPOINT RECORD

EXAMPLE

student name	climate choice	checkpoint 1 notes	checkpoint 2 notes	checkpoint 3 notes
1. Michael	averages 18-75°F 23-30" precip.	Finished portfolio section 1. Great start!		
2. Alysssa	averages 50-90°F 13-20" precip.	Finished portfolio section 1 and reflection.		
3. Brian	averages 22-79°F 23-34" precip.	Finished portfolio section 1. Alex will assist Brian with diorama. Check back.		
4. Alex	averages 0-50°F 23-40" precip.	Finished portfolio section 1 and reflection. Looks good!		
5. Lauren	averages 35-89°F 20-25" precip.	Finished through physical map. Working on road map. Needs a binder.		
6. Brendan	averages 50-100°F 10-18" precip.	Finished portfolio section 1 and reflection. Discussed diorama box choices.		
7. Ella	averages 40-95°F 18-24" precip.	Finished through safety signs. Excellent!		
8. Teagan	averages 10-70°F 27-33" precip.	Finished portfolio section 1. Great start!		
9. Earl	averages 55-112°F 11-20" precip.	Finished through diorama. Looks good!		
10.				

STEP 5
Preparing for the Project Expo and the Classroom Presentations

IMPORTANT!

The expo is an extremely important part of the Envision experience. While it requires a certain amount of work, it solidifies the entire experience for you, your students, and your students' parents. It is very important that students have a special opportunity to shine and display all of the hard work they have done over the quarter. It is also extremely rewarding for you, who will not only be proud of the student accomplishments, but will also receive a lot of parent feedback at this time.

Preparation for the Project Expo:

5.1 Copy one Student Expo Invitation and use your Teacher Planning Guide to complete the expo information.

5.2 For each Envision student, copy a completed expo invitation and fold it accordingly.

Invite Families to the Project Expo:

5.3 Give a Student Expo Invitation to each Envision student. Point out to the students that there is an Expo Invitation Response included with the invitation for each family to sign, detach, and return.

5.4 Send the Student Expo Invitations home with the students to their families.

Preparation for the Project Expo Continued:

5.5 As the expo responses are returned to you, record the information in the correct columns of the Teacher Forms Checklist.

5.6 Based on the Expo Invitation Responses, review whether any students will need special equipment, such as a computer or television. Reserve the equipment if necessary.

5.7 Based on the Expo Invitation Responses, find and reserve a large enough expo location (classroom, library, gymnasium, or hallway) in which to host the expo. Be sure the location can accommodate any equipment required by the students.

5.8 Create a general plan for ordering, obtaining, and serving refreshments (optional).

5.9 Copy a Student Certificate for each Envision student. Complete the certificates and set them aside for the Project Expo.

5.10 Copy a Student Name Sign for each Envision student. Complete each name sign and set it aside for the Project Expo.

5.11 Walk the route from the entrance of the Project Expo location building to the entrance of the Project Expo location itself. Count the number of Left and Right Arrow Signs you will need to post along the way. Make enough copies of each and set them aside for the Project Expo.

TEACHER INSTRUCTION GUIDE

Preparation for Classroom Presentations and the Project Expo:

5.12 Copy a Teacher Assessment for each Envision student to use for Classroom Presentations.

5.13 Copy a Student Self-Assessment for each Envision student. Set them aside for Student Self-Assessment time.

IMPORTANT!

Be sure to keep the Student Self-Assessments separate from the Teacher Assessments. The main reason for this is so that students are assessing themselves without seeing the points you have already given. Students cannot complete their Self-Assessments prior to your Teacher Assessments because they need to wait until after they have given their Classroom Presentations.

5.14 Confirm your room and equipment reservations for the Project Expo.

5.15 Purchase any optional supplies or refreshments you will need for the Project Expo.

BACKYARD GETAWAY

YOU'RE INVITED!

envision

EXPO INVITATION RESPONSE

Please fill out and return by: *Friday, Nov. 2*

Student Name: _____

Student Attending? ☐ Yes ☐ No

Number of Student Guests Attending: _____

Will your child need any special school equipment for the expo (i.e., computer or TV)? Please List: _____

_____

Thank you.

We look forward to seeing you at this special event!

BACKYARD GETAWAY

PLEASE JOIN US FOR OUR ENVISION BACKYARD GETAWAY EXPO!

Why? *To view students' Envision accomplishments*

Who? *All are welcome - family and friends*

Where? *Mind Vine Elementary Gymnasium*

When? *Wednesday, Nov. 7, 2XXX · 6:30 pm - 7:30 pm*

Remember to bring your camera!

BACKYARD GETAWAY

CERTIFICATE OF ACHIEVEMENT

Michael

AWARDED TO

November 7, 2XXX

DATE

Mrs. Bondy

SIGNATURE

envisi⦿n

BACKYARD GETAWAY PROJECT

Michael

STUDENT

envisi⦿n

TEACHER ASSESSMENT
TEACHER ASSESSMENT

TEACHER ASSESSMENT

Component 1: Building Your Project Portfolio
Total Possible Portfolio Points: 79 out of 100 total possible for project

Requirements	Possible Points	Teacher Points	Average Points
Portfolio Section 1: Climate and Terrain Features			
1. Computer-Generated Climate and Terrain Features Table: Analyze the range of different climates and terrain features found in your state or country. List three to five climates and terrains that you would enjoy best for your backyard. Create a titled table using the computer showing the characteristics of each climate and terrain.	3		
2. Climate and Terrain Features Choices: Using your features table, highlight a specific climate and one or two terrain features that you will choose for your backyard. Explain your reasoning in making these choices.	2		
3. Physical Map: Create a physical map of your backyard. Your backyard can have any shape you like as long as it remains a total of one acre in size – no larger, no smaller. Find the conversion for an acre into square feet or square yards and include a scale with your map. Label the terrain features in your yard, keeping them to scale. Be sure to include a creative map title and a key. Refine this map as you progress through the upcoming objectives.	4		
4. Road Map: Create a road map of your backyard using the computer or a pencil and paper. Draw and label the area locations in your yard as you work on the upcoming objectives. Create a key with symbols if needed. Be sure to include your creative map title and map scale. Refine this map as needed.	4		
Portfolio Section 2: Area Locations			
1. Relaxation Area Reflection: Reflect on and make an unlimited list of activities and items that are relaxing to you. They may be activities such as reading, music, or exercise. They may be items such as foods, types of art, or animals. Look over your list. Record ways to incorporate them into your backyard relaxation area and explain why you chose them.	3		
2. Relaxation Area Diorama: Create a diorama of how your relaxation area will look. Include all of the activities and other items you chose in number one above. Be creative, detailed, colorful, and include labels.	5		
3. Recreation Area Brainstorm: Brainstorm recreational activities that you enjoy or would like to enjoy. Some activity examples are: volleyball, croquet, swimming, ice-skating, bug collecting, bird watching, or rock wall climbing. Record creative ways that you could incorporate two to five of them in your backyard recreation area.	3		
4. Recreation Area Safety Rules Signs: For each of your backyard recreational activities, design a safety rules sign. Each titled sign should list important rules for being safe and playing fair with each of your recreational activities.	5		

STUDENT SELF-ASSESSMENT
STUDENT SELF-ASSESSMENT

STUDENT SELF-ASSESSMENT

Component 1: Building Your Project Portfolio
Total Possible Portfolio Points: 79 out of 100 total possible for project

Requirements	Possible Points	Student Points
Portfolio Section 1: Climate and Terrain Features		
1. Computer-Generated Climate and Terrain Features Table: Analyze the range of different climates and terrain features found in your state or country. List three to five climates and terrains that you would enjoy best for your backyard. Create a titled table using the computer showing the characteristics of each climate and terrain.	3	
2. Climate and Terrain Features Choices: Using your features table, highlight a specific climate and one or two terrain features that you will choose for your backyard. Explain your reasoning in making these choices.	2	
3. Physical Map: Create a physical map of your backyard. Your backyard can have any shape you like as long as it remains a total of one acre in size – no larger, no smaller. Find the conversion for an acre into square feet or square yards and include a scale with your map. Label the terrain features in your yard, keeping them to scale. Be sure to include a creative map title and a key. Refine this map as you progress through the upcoming objectives.	4	
4. Road Map: Create a road map of your backyard using the computer or a pencil and paper. Draw and label the area locations in your yard as you work on the upcoming objectives. Create a key with symbols if needed. Be sure to include your creative map title and map scale. Refine this map as needed.	4	
Portfolio Section 2: Area Locations		
1. Relaxation Area Reflection: Reflect on and make an unlimited list of activities and items that are relaxing to you. They may be activities such as reading, music, or exercise. They may be items such as foods, types of art, or animals. Look over your list. Record ways to incorporate them into your backyard relaxation area and explain why you chose them.	3	
2. Relaxation Area Diorama: Create a diorama of how your relaxation area will look. Include all of the activities and other items you chose in number one above. Be creative, detailed, colorful, and include labels.	5	
3. Recreation Area Brainstorm: Brainstorm recreational activities that you enjoy or would like to enjoy. Some activity examples are: volleyball, croquet, swimming, ice-skating, bug collecting, bird watching, or rock wall climbing. Record creative ways that you could incorporate two to five of them in your backyard recreation area.	3	
4. Recreation Area Safety Rules Signs: For each of your backyard recreational activities, design a safety rules sign. Each titled sign should list important rules for being safe and playing fair with each of your recreational activities.	5	

STEP 6
Conducting the Classroom Presentations

This is the first occasion for your Envision students to share their completed projects with an audience – in this case, you and the rest of the class. It is the only opportunity they will have to formally present their projects to an audience.

Note: For logistics and classroom management reasons, choose the Option below that best describes your Envision student participation and follow its set of directions.

Classroom Presentations Option A:
A minority of the class is participating in Envision

6A.1 When students arrive at school on Classroom Presentation day, have them place their materials in a safe location.

6A.2 Just before you are ready to begin the presentations, gather a pen and the Teacher Assessments that you copied in Step 5.

Note: This will be your only opportunity to assess the presentations. However, you will have more time later to assess the exhibits.

6A.3 Set a table in the front of the room.

6A.4 Ask all students to sit at their regular classroom seats and face the front of the room.

6A.5 Sit in a location that will not be distracting to the presenter or the audience, yet will allow you to assess each presentation and each exhibit item clearly.

6A.6 The First Presenter: Ask for a volunteer or select a student to begin presenting. The student who will present should carry her portfolio and exhibit components to the front of the room and set them on the table. (Enlist another student to help if necessary.)

6A.7 Record the presenting student's name on a Teacher Assessment.

6A.8 Have the student stand to the side of her project and begin her presentation.

6A.9 Assess the student's presentation using a Teacher Assessment.

IMPORTANT!

This will be your only opportunity to assess the presentation.

6A.10 Use any extra time during the presentation to begin assessing the student's exhibit components.

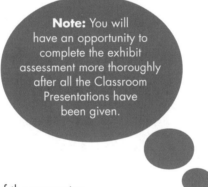

Note: You will have an opportunity to complete the exhibit assessment more thoroughly after all the Classroom Presentations have been given.

6A.11 Allow peers to ask questions of the presenter.

6A.12 Transitioning Between Presenters:
When the first presenter concludes her presentation and everyone has finished applauding, ask for the next volunteer or call the next student's name. As the next student is gathering his materials, the first student can remove hers and set them back where they had been placed earlier. Allow a minute or two for transitioning. Continue this process until all of your Envision students have presented.

6A.13 Conclude the presentations by thanking your Envision students for all of their hard work and by thanking all students for their attention.

Classroom Presentations Option B:
A majority or all of the class is participating in Envision

6B.1 When students arrive at school on Classroom Presentation day, have them place their materials in a safe location.

6B.2 Just before you are ready to begin the presentations, gather a pen, the Teacher Assessments (copied in Step 5), and a clipboard or other writing surface to carry with you.

6B.3 Instruct all Envision students to set up their portfolios and exhibits at their desks. This should take just a few minutes.

6B.4 The First Presenter: Ask for a volunteer or select a student to begin presenting.

6B.5 Record the presenting student's name on an assessment, using your clipboard for writing support.

6B.6 Have the student remain at her seat and stand to the side of her project. Ask all other students to quietly gather in front of her.

6B.7 Stand in a location that will not be distracting to the presenter or the audience, yet will allow you to assess each presentation and each exhibit item clearly.

6B.8 Allow the student to begin her presentation.

6B.9 Assess the student's presentation using a Teacher Assessment.

IMPORTANT!

This will be your only opportunity to assess the presentation.

6B.10 Use any extra time during the presentation to begin assessing her exhibit components.

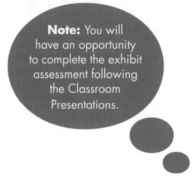

Note: You will have an opportunity to complete the exhibit assessment following the Classroom Presentations.

6B.11 Transitioning Between Presenters: When the first presenter concludes her presentation and everyone has finished applauding, ask for the next volunteer or call the next student's name. Direct everyone to quietly move to that student's exhibit. Continue this process until all of your Envision students have presented.

6B.12 Conclude the presentations by thanking your Envision students for all of their hard work and by thanking all students for their attention. Keep all projects set up as you will now be conducting the Classroom Expo.

STEP 7

Classroom Expo & Student Self-Assessment

The Classroom Expo is a time where classroom peers have a chance to walk around and view the projects. Each Envision student will stand with his project and answer any questions that his peers may have. This will now be your opportunity to further assess the exhibit components. Again, for logistics and classroom management reasons, choose the option below that best describes your Envision student participation and follow its set of directions.

Classroom Expo and Student Self-Assessment
Option A: A minority of the class is participating in Envision

7A.1 Just before you are ready to begin the Classroom Expo, gather a pen, the Teacher Assessments (copied in Step 5), and a clipboard or other writing surface to carry with you.

7A.2 Direct your non-Envision students to remain seated at their desks.

7A.3 Have your Envision students quietly set up their portfolios and exhibits. This can be done at a single large table, on a counter space, or at each student's desk.

7A.4 Have each Envision student stand beside her exhibit.

7A.5 Instruct the rest of the class to put away their work materials and begin visiting each Envision exhibit. Encourage them to ask questions about the projects. Tell them the approximate amount of time they will have to visit all the exhibits.

7A.6 While students are enjoying the Classroom Expo, walk around the room and assess each student's exhibit components using your clipboard, pen, and Teacher Assessments.

IMPORTANT!

Students will be leaving their exhibits in the classroom until they set up for the Project Expo. Therefore, if you need more time to assess the exhibits, you may continue the assessments at another time prior to the expo.

7A.7 At the Classroom Expo conclusion, ask non-Envision students to return to their desks. Allow your Envision students a few minutes to take down their exhibits and return them to a safe location.

7A.8 Have Envision students return to their desks.

7A.9 Distribute the Student Self-Assessments (copied in Step 5) to Envision students and have the students privately complete them, including adding the total points for each component. Instruct the students to hand them in to you when they are finished.

Classroom Expo and Student Self-Assessment
Option B: A majority or all of the class is participating in Envision

7B.1 Continue to carry your clipboard, pen, and Teacher Assessments to use during the Classroom Expo.

7B.2 Direct half of your Envision students to stand beside their exhibits.

7B.3 Instruct the rest of the class to begin visiting each Envision exhibit. Encourage them to ask questions about the projects. Tell them the approximate amount of time they will have to visit all the exhibits.

7B.4 While students are enjoying the Classroom Expo, walk around the room and assess the vacant student exhibits using your clipboard, pen, and Teacher Assessments.

7B.5 When you are ready to move on to the second set of exhibits, direct your students to switch roles. Any non-Envision students can continue visiting exhibits they have not yet been to.

7B.6 Again, proceed with the Classroom Expo remembering to tell students the approximate amount of time they will have to visit the remaining exhibits.

7B.7 During this time, walk around the room and assess the remaining student exhibits.

IMPORTANT!

Students will be leaving their exhibits in the classroom until they set up for the Project Expo. Therefore, if you need more time to assess the exhibits, you may continue the assessments at another time prior to the expo.

7B.8 At the Classroom Expo conclusion, ask students to help one another take down their exhibits and return them to a safe location. Non-Envision students can help with this as well.

7B.9 Have all students return to their desks.

7B.10 Distribute the Student Self-Assessments (copied in Step 5) to Envision students and have the students privately complete them, including adding the total points for each component. Instruct the students to hand them in to you when they are finished.

STEP 8

Final Preparation for the Project Expo

Students take immense pride in sharing the fruits of their hard work with relatives and friends at the Project Expo. The expo offers a fun, festive environment where family and friends have the opportunity to meet all the Envision students and see their projects. It is also a forum for Envision students to share their project experiences and educational growth with guests.

Final Preparation for the Project Expo:

8.1 Ensure that tables, desks, chairs, refreshments, and any special equipment are in place. Refer to your Teacher Forms Checklist for any special equipment needed.

8.2 Prepare and set aside a camera, and video recorder if desired, for your use at the expo.

8.3 Assign each student a location for exhibit setup.

8.4 Place the appropriate Student Name Sign (prepared in Step 5) at each student's exhibit area.

8.5 Allow small groups of students to take their project components to their designated exhibit areas.

8.6 Hang the Envision Poster at the entrance of the expo location building.

8.7 Hang the Expo Arrow Signs (prepared in Step 5) along the route from the entrance of the location building to the specific expo location itself.

8.8 Hang the Project Poster at the entrance to the Project Expo location.

8.9 Have the Student Certificates (prepared in Step 5) ready to present to the students at the expo.

8.10 Explain to students that they should be on their best behavior at the expo. Also explain that each student should remain at his or her exhibit for the majority of the expo to answer guests' project questions.

welcome

BACKYA...

envision®

An inspirational real-world program for gifted learners

BACKYARD GETAWAY

ENVIRONMENTAL DECLARATION

CIVIC MISSION

FITNESS PURSUIT

STEP 9

The Project Expo:

9.1 Greet the students and guests as they enter the expo location. Ask students to go directly to their exhibits. Invite guests to explore and ask questions at each exhibit.

9.2 Be sure to take photos, and video if desired, of the expo. Obtain at least one photo of each student with his exhibit to post later on your project bulletin board. Also, the photos may come in handy if you need to double-check anything during your final project assessment.

9.3 After everyone has had time to view the projects, gather them together and formally present the Student Certificates to the Envision students. Thank everyone for attending and for supporting the hard work of the students. Ask the Envision students to take home all of their project components except for the portfolios. You will need to assess these, and you will return them with each student's final Teacher Assessment.

9.4 Collect the portfolios so that you can complete the Teacher Assessment for each project.

STEP 10

Conclusion, Teacher Assessment, and Student Review

Conclusion and Teacher Assessment:

10.1 Develop all expo photos.

10.2 Hang the Envision Bulletin Board Banner on a bulletin board in a high-traffic area.

10.3 Pick up the Envision photos and arrange them on the bulletin board. This will show the students your pride in their work.

10.4 Referring to student portfolios, complete the "Teacher Points" column for the "Component 1: Building Your Project Portfolio" section of the Teacher Assessments.

10.5 Add all columns on each Teacher Assessment, recording the "Total Points" for each component along with the "Total Project Points" at the end of the assessment.

10.6 Average the amount of each "Total Points" section from each student's Student Self-Assessment with the corresponding "Total Points" amount for each component section on his or her Teacher Assessment.

10.7 Record each component's average amount in the "Average Points" column of the Teacher Assessment for each student

10.8 For each student, record the "Total Project Points" in your personal record book. Staple each student's Student Self-Assessment to their Teacher Assessment. Copy these packets for your records.

Student Review:

10.9 Return each student's portfolio and completed assessment packet.

10.10 Allow the students time to review their assessment packets and ask questions if they wish.

CONGRATULATIONS
ON PROJECT COMPLETION!

APPENDIX 1:
BACKYARD GETAWAY FORMS
AND RESOURCE CARDS

Levels From Lowest to Highest:
KNOWLEDGE • COMPREHENSION • APPLICATION • ANALYSIS • EVALUATION • SYNTHESIS

Below you will find each Backyard Getaway requirement, along with its corresponding level of Bloom's Taxonomy.

> **IMPORTANT!**
> The levels listed above are cumulative. For example, the highest level of thinking, Synthesis, incorporates all other levels of thinking: Knowledge, Comprehension, Application, Analysis, and Evaluation.

COMPONENT 1
Building Your Project Portfolio Total Possible Portfolio Points: 79 out of 100 total possible for project

Portfolio Section 1: Climate and Terrain Features

1. Computer-Generated Climate and Terrain Features Table (3 points): Analyze the range of different climates and terrain features found in your state or country. **ANALYSIS** List three to five climates and terrains that you would enjoy best for your backyard. **EVALUATION** Create a titled table using the computer showing the characteristics of each climate and terrain. **SYNTHESIS**

2. Climate and Terrain Features Choices (2 points): Using your features table, highlight a specific climate and one or two terrain features that you will choose for your backyard. Explain your reasoning in making these choices. **EVALUATION**

3. Physical Map (4 points): Create a physical map of your backyard. Your backyard can have any shape you like as long as it remains a total of one acre in size – no larger, no smaller. **SYNTHESIS** Find the conversion for an acre into square feet or square yards and include a scale with your map. **COMPREHENSION** Label the terrain features in your yard, keeping them to scale. Be sure to include a creative map title and a key. Refine this map as you progress through the upcoming objectives. **SYNTHESIS**

4. Road Map (4 points): Create a road map of your backyard using the computer or a pencil and paper. Draw and label the area locations in your yard as you work on the upcoming objectives. Create a key with symbols if needed. Be sure to include your creative map title and map scale. Refine this map as needed. **SYNTHESIS**

Portfolio Section 2: Area Locations

1. Relaxation Area Reflection (3 points): Reflect on and make an unlimited list of activities and items that are relaxing to you. They may be activities such as reading, music, or exercise. They may be items such as foods, types of art, or animals. **EVALUATION** Look over your list. Record ways to incorporate them into your backyard relaxation area and explain why you chose them. **SYNTHESIS**

2. Relaxation Area Diorama (5 points): Create a diorama of how your relaxation area will look. Include all of the activities and other items you chose in number one above. Be creative, detailed, colorful, and include labels. This diorama will be kept separate from your portfolio. **SYNTHESIS**

3. Recreation Area Brainstorm (3 points): Brainstorm recreational activities that you enjoy or would like to enjoy. Some activity examples are: volleyball, croquet, swimming, ice-skating, bug collecting, bird watching, or rock wall climbing. **EVALUATION** Record creative ways that you could incorporate two to five of them in your backyard recreation area. **SYNTHESIS**

4. Recreation Area Safety Rules Signs (5 points): For each of your backyard recreational activities, design a safety rules sign. Each titled sign should list important rules for being safe and playing fair with each of your recreational activities. **SYNTHESIS**

5. Water Habitat Watercolor (5 points): Research various types of water habitats and the ecosystems found within each. Choose the water habitat you would like to have in your backyard. **EVALUATION** Create a watercolor artwork of your water habitat. Be sure to include all plant and animal life in and around your water habitat. **SYNTHESIS**

6. Water Habitat Food Chain (5 points): Choose a specific animal at the bottom or top of a food chain in your water habitat. Find or create pictures of the other animals in that food chain. Organize them into a visual food chain chart complete with arrows, labels, and a title. **SYNTHESIS**

7. Water Cycle Poem (5 points): Use the computer to compose a poem about your water habitat and how it is affected by each phase of the water cycle. Give your poem a title. **SYNTHESIS**

8. Flower or Food Garden T-Chart and Choice (4 points): Make a titled two-column t-chart with the headings "Flower Garden" and "Food Garden". Below each column title, list positive and negative aspects of having each. **SYNTHESIS** Based on your chart, choose whether you would like to have a flower garden or a food garden in your backyard. Explain your decision below the chart. **EVALUATION**

9. Flower or Food Garden Flipbook (7 points): When planting a garden, it is helpful to have easy-to-access information about each plant that you grow. By creating a flipbook of information about each of the plants in your garden, you will have a handy reference tool that you can expand as your garden expands. Follow the steps below to create a customized flipbook showcasing the plants in your garden.

Step 1, Flower or Food Garden Page Set-Up: List at least ten flowers or foods you will grow in your garden. **EVALUATION** Be sure they are plants that will thrive in your chosen climate. Record each plant's name on a blank sheet of paper. **COMPREHENSION**

Step 2, Flower or Food Garden Care: Read about your garden plants and record important care information about each on its corresponding sheet of paper from Step 1. Be sure to locate information about maintenance, optimal soil conditions, spacing, planting depth, and amount of sunlight needed. **COMPREHENSION** Also record any other information you feel is important. Include your reference sources on each page. **EVALUATION**

Step 3, Flower or Food Garden Pictures: Adhere a photo or illustration of each plant to the bottom of its respective page. **KNOWLEDGE**

Step 4, Flipbook Assembly: Organize your finished flower or food garden pages into a flipbook. Divide your pages into subgroups to create different sections in your flipbook. Include a table of contents. Make a creative cover for your book with a special name for your garden. This flipbook will be kept separate from your portfolio. **SYNTHESIS**

10. Flower or Food Garden Interdependence Fictional Story (5 points): Research more plants or animals that might be found in your backyard. Write a fictional story that includes important story elements and incorporates the animals' interdependence. Be creative and title your story. **SYNTHESIS**

11. State or Country Tribute Cards (7 points): Follow the steps below to generate state or country tribute cards that highlight various aspects of your state or country.

Step 1, State or Country Tribute Area Research: Research any aspect of your state's or country's history that interests you. Take notes in your own words on the information you find. **COMPREHENSION** Your notes should contain the information that you think is most interesting about the topic. Read the steps below before you begin so that you can organize and record your notes in an efficient manner. Be sure to reference your sources for the information you obtain. **EVALUATION**

Step 2, State or Country Tribute Subtopic Card Set-Up: Organize your notes into four or more subtopics and give each subtopic a title. Record each subtopic title on the top line of a five-by-eight-inch index card. **SYNTHESIS**

Step 3, State or Country Tribute Paragraphs: Using each set of subtopic notes, write at least one formal paragraph about each subtopic. Write each paragraph on the lines below the corresponding subtopic title on each index card you set up in Step 2. Be sure your paragraphs relate to the main state or country aspect you originally researched, and that they are written in your own words. These finalized state or country tribute cards will be kept separate from your portfolio. **COMPREHENSION**

12. State or Country Tribute Artworks (7 points): To accompany each of your state or country tribute writings, create a piece of art to display in your backyard state or country tribute area. One of your art pieces must be some type of sculpture. You may use any medium or combination of media you wish. Media might include: naturally found materials, recycled materials, household items, clay, or papier-mâché. Be creative and have fun with these artworks! These artworks will be kept separate from your portfolio. **SYNTHESIS**

Remaining Portfolio Materials

1. Table of Contents (2 points): Write a table of contents that lists all the sections of your portfolio along with their corresponding page numbers. **COMPREHENSION**

2. Cover Page (1 point): Create an eye-catching cover page for your portfolio that includes an original title for your project as well as your name and the Classroom Presentation date. **SYNTHESIS**

3. Portfolio (2 points): Organize all of your materials in a three-ring binder. The table of contents should come first, followed by your work from Portfolio Sections 1 and 2 above in the order presented. Your cover page should go on the front of the portfolio. **SYNTHESIS**

COMPONENT 2

Creating Your Project Exhibit Total Possible Exhibit Points: 15 out of 100 total possible for project

1. State or Country Tribute Mini Museum (2 points): Arrange your state or country tribute artworks with their written accompaniments to create a miniature museum within your exhibit. **SYNTHESIS**

2. Backyard Getaway Model (7 points): Create a miniature model of your backyard. Label each area location from Portfolio Section 2 and make it as detailed and creative as possible. **SYNTHESIS**

3. Display Board (3 points): Use a large two- or three-panel display board to create an "advertisement" for your Backyard Getaway. It must include your project's title and your name. You may then choose to add any of the required items or any additional materials that you wish. **SYNTHESIS**

4. Exhibit (3 points): Arrange your portfolio, relaxation area diorama, flower or food garden flipbook, state or country mini museum, Backyard Getaway model, and any additional materials you wish to include in an appealing and informative way. **SYNTHESIS**

COMPONENT 3:

Giving Your Classroom Presentation

Total Possible Classroom Presentation Points: 6 out of 100 total possible for project

1. What to Include in Your Presentation:

- Climate and Terrain Features Choices (1 point): Share your climate and terrain features choices. Explain your reasoning for making those choices. **COMPREHENSION**

- Maps (2 points): Display your physical map and road map while explaining the features of each. **COMPREHENSION**

- Area Highlights (1 point): Explain one component from each of your backyard areas, pointing to any relevant materials in your exhibit. **COMPREHENSION**

- Portfolio (1 point): Show your portfolio and explain one component that you would like to highlight. **EVALUATION**

- Mini Museum (1 point): Show and explain the components of your state or country mini museum. **COMPREHENSION**

Step Number	Form Title	Number of Copies
1.1	Teacher Planning Guide	1 only
2.1-2.3	Parent Envision Introduction Letter Parent Backyard Getaway Introduction Letter Student Backyard Getaway Introduction Letter Student Instruction Guide	1 completed, then 1 per student 1 completed, then 1 per student 1 completed only 1 only
3.1-3.4	Teacher Forms Checklist Student Commitment Contract	1 completed only 1 completed, then 1 per student
3.5	Student Backyard Getaway Introduction Letter* Student Instruction Guide* Backyard Getaway Resource Card Appendix Pages*	1 completed, then one per student 1 per student 1 per student (optional)
4.1-4.2	Student Checkpoint Organizer Teacher Checkpoint Record	1 per student 1 completed only
5.1-5.2	Student Expo Invitation	1 completed, then one per student
5.9-5.11	Student Certificate Student Name Sign Left Arrow Sign Right Arrow Sign	1 per student, then each completed 1 per student, then each completed Amount needed Amount needed
5.12-5.13	Teacher Assessment Student Self-Assessment	1 per student 1 per student

* Staple these items into a packet for each student

Events scheduled with the class are in black.

Week	Event (Step Numbers)	Day and Date	Time
1	Planning and Preparing for the Quarter (1.1-1.2)		
	Prepare for Backyard Getaway Introduction (2.1-2.3)		
	Backyard Getaway Introduction (2.4-2.7)		
	Preparation for Backyard Getaway Implementation (3.1-3.6)		
	Backyard Getaway Implementation (3.7-3.17)		
3	Preparation for the Checkpoint Meetings (4.1-4.2)		
	Distribute Checkpoint Organizers (4.3-4.6)		
	Checkpoint Meetings (4.7-4.12)		
5	Preparation for the Checkpoint Meetings (4.1-4.2)		
	Distribute Checkpoint Organizers (4.3-4.6)		
	Checkpoint Meetings (4.7-4.12)		
7	Preparation for the Checkpoint Meetings (4.1-4.2)		
	Distribute Checkpoint Organizers (4.3-4.6)		
	Checkpoint Meetings (4.7-4.12)		
8	Preparation for the Backyard Getaway Expo (5.1-5.2)		
	Invite Families to the Backyard Getaway Expo (5.3-5.4)		
	Preparation for the Backyard Getaway Expo Ctd. (5.5-5.11)		
9	Preparation for Classroom Presentations and the Backyard Getaway Expo (5.12-5.15)		
	Classroom Presentations (6A.1-6A.13 or 6B.1-6B.12)		
	Classroom Expo and Student Self-Assessment (7A.1-7A.9 or 7B.1-7B.10)		
10	Final Preparation for Backyard Getaway Expo (8.1-8.10)		
	Backyard Getaway Expo (9.1-9.4)		
	Conclusion and Teacher Assessment (10.1-10.8)		
	Student Review (10.9-10.10)		

Dear Parent(s),

I am happy to inform you that your child has been invited to participate in an advanced academic program called Envision. I am sending you this letter to explain the program and ask for your permission to include your child in this special opportunity.

Envision is an exciting, yearlong program designed for students who are not sufficiently challenged by the standard grade-level curriculum. The focus of the program is on developing high-level critical thinking and creativity, and encourages students to *envision* how they might achieve their goals for the future. Envision guides students through four real-world-based projects, one for each quarter of the school year.

In chronological order, the four projects are: Backyard Getaway, Environmental Declaration, Civic Mission, and Fitness Pursuit. Backyard Getaway allows students to design a complete, personalized dream backyard using one acre of land. Environmental Declaration is designed to create a deep awareness about a state or national environmental issue and allow students a voice in the matter. The third project, Civic Mission, allows students to interact and learn within their community while performing a service. Finally, Fitness Pursuit energizes students with the opportunity to cultivate an in-depth awareness of healthy habits to live by. Each project introduces new ideas, new vocabulary, new technology, and new challenges.

Students will work on Envision during class time, free time, and at home.

To give permission for your child to participate in Envision, simply sign the Envision Permission Form at the bottom of this letter, detach it, and return the form to me. If you want your child to participate in Envision, please read the attached Parent Backyard Getaway Introduction Letter. The letter introduces you to the first project, informs you of important dates, and requests permission for your child's continued participation. You will receive a Parent Project Introduction Letter at the beginning of each quarter with the start of each new project.

Envision promises to be a wonderful learning opportunity for your child. I look forward to hearing from you. Please feel free to contact me if you have any questions.

Sincerely,

_____

_____

- -

 permission form

Please fill out this section, detach, and return as soon as possible.   Date: _____

❑ I have read the Parent Envision Introduction Letter and give my child permission to participate in the Envision program.

❑ I have read the Parent Envision Introduction Letter and do not give my child permission to participate in the Envision program.

Child's Name:_____   Parent's Signature: _____

BACKYARD GETAWAY

parent backyard getaway introduction letter

Dear Parent(s),

Welcome to Backyard Getaway, the first of four Envision projects that will challenge and inspire your child. Backyard Getaway will immediately engage your child as its challenge is to design a complete, personalized dream backyard using one acre of land.

For this project, your child will research and make decisions in order to create and develop five specific areas within his or her backyard: a relaxation area, a recreation area, a water habitat, a flower or food garden, and a state or country tribute area. Your child will create a table, maps, a personal reflection, safety signs, a watercolor, a food chain, a poem, a t-chart, and a fictional story. All of these written materials will be collected in a portfolio. Next, your child will build an exhibit including a display board, diorama, flipbook, miniature museum, backyard model, and finishing touches that highlight key aspects of the backyard. Lastly, your child will give a brief formal presentation to the class.

A Student Instruction Guide will be provided to guide your child, step by step, through this process. The Instruction Guide is a comprehensive list of project requirements and is designed to engage higher-level thinking. The guide also references helpful Resource Cards, which provide additional explanations, ideas, tips, and directions. There will be a set of these cards in our classroom to which your child can refer.

Backyard Getaway is designed to be worked on independently during class time, free time, and at home. By scheduling several Checkpoint Meeting dates throughout the quarter, I will be able to monitor each student's progress. On these dates, I will meet with each student to discuss accomplishments and plan goals for the next checkpoint. I will also address any difficulties students might be having.

Backyard Getaway will conclude with a Project Expo. The expo will be your child's opportunity to share his or her finished project with family, friends, and other guests. You will receive a detailed invitation to the Project Expo later in the quarter.

Dates to Remember:

Checkpoint 1: _____

Checkpoint 2: _____

Checkpoint 3: _____

Classroom Presentation: _____

Backyard Getaway Expo: _____ , _____

Sincerely,

_____

_____

BACKYARD GETAWAY

student backyard getaway introduction letter

Dear Student,

Welcome to Backyard Getaway! This is the first of four projects you will embark on as part of the Envision Program experience. Backyard Getaway is about creating a paradise escape or a place you can get away to whenever you like. It is also a journey of discovery, research, and creativity.

The project begins with your receiving an imaginary plot of land measuring one acre in size. Keeping this size in mind, you will create five unique areas within your backyard: a relaxation area, a recreation area, a water habitat, a flower or food garden, and a state or country tribute area. For this project, you have no budget; the sky is the limit!

Backyard Getaway contains four components. The first will be to conduct research and create numerous components for your backyard areas. You will organize this information in a project portfolio. The second will be to create an exhibit that displays additional backyard components you will create. The third will be to share your completed portfolio and exhibit with your classmates. To do this you will give a brief formal presentation. During your presentation you will explain key aspects of your Backyard Getaway. Last will be the Project Expo, an event that celebrates your hard work and achievements. This final component allows you the opportunity to invite family and friends to share in your success.

You will work on Backyard Getaway throughout the school day, during your free time, and at home. Generally, you will be expected to work on your own. You will consult with me periodically at Checkpoint Meetings to discuss your progress and receive guidance. Between the checkpoints, feel free to discuss your project with other Envision students.

The attached Student Instruction Guide contains all the information you will need to complete the required Backyard Getaway Project successfully. The Instruction Guide will challenge you to be resourceful, organized, and to think at a higher level.

Dates to Remember:

Checkpoint 1: _____

Checkpoint 2: _____

Checkpoint 3: _____

Classroom Presentation: _____

Backyard Getaway Expo: _____ , _____

After reading this introduction, you are now ready to begin thinking about your Backyard Getaway. Good luck and have fun!

Sincerely,

_____

_____

**Building Your Project Portfolio • Creating Your Project Exhibit
Presenting Your Project • Attending the Expo**

CREATIVITY
IS HIGHLY
ENCOURAGED!

IMPORTANT!

Available resource cards are denoted by a Backyard Getaway icon [icon]. When you see one of these icons, you will know that there is a corresponding resource card available that gives additional helpful information and depicts visual examples for your reference. Also be sure to visit www.mindvinepress.com, other trustworthy Internet sites, and library reference materials for additional resources and examples.

COMPONENT 1

Building Your Project Portfolio Total Possible Portfolio Points: 79 out of 100 total possible for project

Get ready! It is now time to plan and make decisions about the backyard of your dreams. This will be a wonderful experience and opportunity to engage your intellectual abilities as well as your imagination. Complete the numbered requirements below, in order, as they build upon one another and will guide you smoothly through the process. Good luck!

Note: "Component 1: Building Your Backyard Getaway Portfolio" is separated into two sections: "Portfolio Section 1: Climate and Terrain Features" and "Portfolio Section 2: Area Locations".

STUDENT INSTRUCTION GUIDE

Portfolio Section 1: Climate and Terrain Features

1. Computer-Generated Climate and Terrain Features Table (3 points): Analyze the range of different climates and terrain features found in your state or country. List three to five climates and terrains that you would enjoy best for your backyard. Create a titled table using the computer showing the characteristics of each climate and terrain.

2. Climate and Terrain Features Choices (2 points): Using your features table, highlight a specific climate and one or two terrain features that you will choose for your backyard. Explain your reasoning in making these choices.

3. Physical Map (4 points): Create a physical map of your backyard. Your backyard can have any shape you like as long as it remains a total of one acre in size – no larger, no smaller. Find the conversion for an acre into square feet or square yards and include a scale with your map. Label the terrain features in your yard, keeping them to scale. Be sure to include a creative map title and a key. Refine this map as you progress through the upcoming objectives.

4. Road Map (4 points): Create a road map of your backyard using the computer or a pencil and paper. Draw and label the area locations in your yard as you work on the upcoming objectives. Create a key with symbols if needed. Be sure to include your creative map title and map scale. Refine this map as needed.

Portfolio Section 2: Area Locations

Your backyard must contain the following areas: a relaxation area, a recreation area, a water habitat, a flower or food garden, and a state or country tribute area. You may add other areas as you wish.

1. Relaxation Area Reflection (3 points): Reflect on and make an unlimited list of activities and items that are relaxing to you. They may be activities such as reading, music, or exercise. They may be items such as foods, types of art, or animals. Look over your list. Record ways to incorporate them into your backyard relaxation area and explain why you chose them.

2. Relaxation Area Diorama (5 points): Create a diorama of how your relaxation area will look. Include all of the activities and other items you chose in number one above. Be creative, detailed, colorful, and include labels. This diorama will be kept separate from your portfolio.

3. Recreation Area Brainstorm (3 points): Brainstorm recreational activities that you enjoy or would like to enjoy. Some activity examples are: volleyball, croquet, swimming, ice-skating, bug collecting, bird watching, or rock wall climbing. Record creative ways that you could incorporate two to five of them in your backyard recreation area.

4. Recreation Area Safety Rules Signs (5 points): For each of your backyard recreational activities, design a safety rules sign. Each titled sign should list important rules for being safe and playing fair with each of your recreational activities.

5. Water Habitat Watercolor (5 points): Research various types of water habitats and the ecosystems found within each. Choose the water habitat you would like to have in your backyard. Create a watercolor artwork of your water habitat. Be sure to include all plant and animal life in and around your water habitat.

6. Water Habitat Food Chain (5 points): Choose a specific animal at the bottom or top of a food chain in your water habitat. Find or create pictures of the other animals in that food chain. Organize them into a visual food chain chart complete with arrows, labels, and a title.

7. Water Cycle Poem (5 points): Use the computer to compose a poem about your water habitat and how it is affected by each phase of the water cycle. Give your poem a title. It may be written in any style you like.

8. Flower or Food Garden T-Chart and Choice (4 points): Make a titled two-column t-chart with the headings "Flower Garden" and "Food Garden". Below each column title, list positive and negative aspects of having each. Based on your chart, choose whether you would like to have a flower garden or a food garden in your backyard. Explain your decision below the chart.

9. Flower or Food Garden Flipbook (7 points): When planting a garden, it is helpful to have easy-to-access information about each plant that you grow. By creating a flipbook of information about each of the plants in your garden, you will have a handy reference tool that you can expand as your garden expands. Follow the steps below to create a customized flipbook showcasing the plants in your garden.

Step 1, Flower or Food Garden Page Set-Up: List at least ten flowers or foods you will grow in your garden. Be sure they are plants that will thrive in your chosen climate. Record each plant's name on a blank sheet of paper.

Step 2, Flower or Food Garden Care: Read about your garden plants and record important care information about each on its corresponding sheet of paper from Step 1. Be sure to locate information about maintenance, optimal soil conditions, spacing, planting depth, and amount of sunlight needed. Also record any other information you feel is important. Include your reference sources on each page.

Step 3, Flower or Food Garden Pictures: Adhere a photo or illustration of each plant to the bottom of its respective page.

Step 4, Flipbook Assembly: Organize your finished flower or food garden pages into a flipbook. Divide your pages into subgroups to create different sections in your flipbook. Include a table of contents. Make a creative cover for your book with a special name for your garden. This flipbook will be kept separate from your portfolio.

10. Flower or Food Garden Interdependence Fictional Story (5 points): Research more plants or animals that might be found in your backyard. Write a fictional story that includes important story elements and incorporates the animals' interdependence. Be creative and title your story.

11. State or Country Tribute Cards (7 points): Follow the steps below to generate state or country tribute cards that highlight various aspects of your state or country.

Step 1, State or Country Tribute Area Research: Research any aspect of your state's or country's history that interests you. Take notes in your own words on the information you find. Your notes should contain the information that you think is most interesting about the topic. Read the steps below before you begin so that you can organize and record your notes in an efficient manner. Be sure to reference your sources for the information you obtain.

Step 2, State or Country Tribute Subtopic Card Set-Up: Organize your notes into four or more subtopics and give each subtopic a title. Record each subtopic title on the top line of a five-by-eight-inch index card.

Step 3, State or Country Tribute Paragraphs: Using each set of subtopic notes, write at least one formal paragraph about each subtopic. Write each paragraph on the lines below the corresponding subtopic title on each index card you set up in Step 2. Be sure your paragraphs relate to the main state or country aspect you originally researched, and that they are written in your own words. These finalized state or country tribute cards will be kept separate from your portfolio.

12. State or Country Tribute Artworks (7 points): To accompany each of your state or country tribute writings, create a piece of art to display in your backyard state or country tribute area. One of your art pieces must be some type of sculpture. You may use any medium or combination of media you wish. Media might include: naturally found materials, recycled materials, household items, clay, or papier-mâché. Be creative and have fun with these artworks! These artworks will be kept separate from your portfolio.

Remaining Portfolio Materials

1. Table of Contents (2 points): Write a table of contents that lists all the sections of your portfolio along with their corresponding page numbers.

2. Cover Page (1 point): Create an eye-catching cover page for your portfolio that includes an original title for your project as well as your name and the Classroom Presentation date.

3. Portfolio (2 points): Organize all of your materials in a three-ring binder. The table of contents should come first, followed by your work from Portfolio Sections 1 and 2 above in the order presented. Your cover page should go on the front of the portfolio.

STUDENT INSTRUCTION GUIDE

COMPONENT 2

Creating Your Project Exhibit Total Possible Exhibit Points: 15 out of 100 total possible for project

It is now time to design and create an informative and appealing visual exhibit of your Backyard Getaway. The items you complete will be viewed by your classmates on the day of your Classroom Presentation and also by everyone who attends the Backyard Getaway Expo at the end of the term. As always, put your best work into designing, creating, and integrating your exhibit items.

Note:
Keep in mind that each item is only one part of the overall exhibit. In other words, no single item has to say everything about your Backyard Getaway. Decide upon a purpose for each item. Consider how best to arrange your exhibit for the greatest effect.

1. State or Country Tribute Mini Museum (2 points): Arrange your state or country tribute artworks with their written accompaniments to create a miniature museum within your exhibit.

2. Backyard Getaway Model (7 points): Create a miniature model of your backyard. Label each area location from Portfolio Section 2 and make it as detailed and creative as possible.

3. Display Board (3 points): Use a large two- or three-panel display board to create an "advertisement" for your Backyard Getaway. It must include your project's title and your name. You may then choose to add any of the required items or any additional materials that you wish.

4. Exhibit (3 points): Arrange your portfolio, relaxation area diorama, flower or food garden flipbook, state or country mini museum, Backyard Getaway model, and any additional materials you wish to include in an appealing and informative way.

You have now completed Component 2 of the Backyard Getaway Project, an important exhibit that creatively displays your backyard. Now that you have finished your portfolio and exhibit, you are ready to confidently prepare for your Classroom Presentation (Component 3). Enjoy sharing your exciting project with your peers and teacher!

COMPONENT 3:

Giving Your Classroom Presentation
Total Possible Classroom Presentation Points: 6 out of 100 total possible for project

Now that you have planned and developed your Backyard Getaway, it is time to share your creation with others. Your Classroom Presentation is an opportunity to formally present some highlights from your backyard, and to share some of your hard work. Your portfolio and exhibit contain all the information you will need to refer to for the presentation, so relax and have fun with it.

1. 🛬 **What to Include in Your Presentation:**

- Climate and Terrain Features Choices (1 point): Share your climate and terrain features choices. Explain your reasoning for making those choices.

- Maps (2 points): Display your physical map and road map while explaining the features of each.

- Area Highlights (1 point): Explain one component from each of your backyard areas, pointing to any relevant materials in your exhibit.

- Portfolio (1 point): Show your portfolio and explain one component that you would like to highlight.

- Mini Museum (1 point): Show and explain the components of your state or country mini museum.

Note: Your presentation should last between 3-4 minutes and should be rehearsed, but not memorized. If you forget to include information from one of the bullet points, your teacher will ask you the question so that you have a chance to answer it.

Bring to the Classroom Presentation: All of your exhibit items and anything extra that you would like to enhance your exhibit.

You are now finished with Components 1, 2, and 3 – all of the assessed portions of your project. The final Component, Attending the Backyard Getaway Expo, provides a festive closure to the Backyard Getaway Project.

COMPONENT 4:

Attending the Backyard Getaway Expo (The expo does not involve any points.)

Now that you have completed your project and presented it to your peers, it's time to share your work with family and friends at the Backyard Getaway Expo. The expo is an event that recognizes and celebrates the hard work you have done on your Backyard Getaway Project. At the expo, you will set up and stand by your exhibit as invited guests walk around informally and view the projects. Guests may ask you friendly questions about your project as they visit your exhibit, so have fun sharing your Backyard Getaway creation with them.

Bring to the Expo: all of your exhibit items and anything extra that you would like to enhance your exhibit.

CONGRATULATIONS ON YOUR COMPLETED BACKYARD GETAWAY PROJECT!

TEACHER FORMS CHECKLIST

use this checklist to record forms submitted by the students

student name	envision permission form	student commitment contract	student checkpoint organizer 1	student checkpoint organizer 2	student checkpoint organizer 3	expo invitation response number attending special equip.needed
1.						
2.						
3.						
4.						
5.						
6.						
7.						
8.						
9.						
10.						
11.						
12.						
13.						
14.						
15.						
16.						
17.						
18.						
19.						
20.						
21.						
22.						
23.						
24.						
25.						

STUDENT COMMITMENT CONTRACT

expectations

project work time

I agree to:

- be responsible for following my Student Instruction Guide to do my work.
- keep track of all my project materials.
- work hard on Envision without disturbing others.
- save my unanswered questions until my teacher is free to talk.

checkpoint meetings

I will come prepared with:

- my Student Instruction Guide.
- my completed Student Checkpoint Organizer.
- all of my project materials.

important dates and times

Checkpoint 1: _____

Checkpoint 2: _____

Checkpoint 3: _____

Classroom Presentation: _____

Backyard Getaway Expo: _____

_____

signatures

I agree to:

- meet expectations on the dates listed above.
- complete each of the Backyard Getaway requirements to the best of my ability.
- bring my project work to school each day so that I can work on it during extra time.
- take my project work from school each night so that I can work on it at home.

I understand that the Envision Backyard Getaway Project is a special opportunity, and that if I do not meet the above expectations, I may be asked to return to normal classroom activities.

Student Signature: _____ Date: _____

Parent Signature: _____ Date: _____

Please return this contract by: _____

STUDENT CHECKPOINT ORGANIZER

Student Name: _____ Checkpoint Date: _____

Climate Choice: _____

directions

1. Using your Student Instruction Guide check off any requirements that you have completed up to this point.

2. Bring the following items to the Checkpoint Meeting:

• your Student Instruction Guide.

• your completed Student Checkpoint Organizer.

• all of your project materials.

questions

1. Which requirements have you completed up to this point?

_____

_____

2. Is there anything you need help with?

_____

_____

3. Is there anything else about your project that you would like to discuss?

_____

_____

4. List at least three goals you expect to accomplish by the next checkpoint.

_____

_____

TEACHER CHECKPOINT RECORD

student name	climate choice	checkpoint 1 notes	checkpoint 2 notes	checkpoint 3 notes
1.				
2.				
3.				
4.				
5.				
6.				
7.				
8.				
9.				
10.				

YOU'RE INVITED!

BACKYARD GETAWAY

EXPO INVITATION RESPONSE

Please fill out and return by: _____

Student Name: _____

Student Attending? ☐ Yes ☐ No

Number of Student Guests Attending: _____

Will your child need any special school equipment for the expo (i.e., computer or TV)? Please List: _____

_____

Thank you.

We look forward to seeing you at this special event!

BACKYARD GETAWAY

PLEASE JOIN US FOR OUR ENVISION BACKYARD GETAWAY EXPO!

Why? _____

Who? _____

Where? _____

When? _____

Remember to bring your camera!

BACKYARD GETAWAY

CERTIFICATE OF ACHIEVEMENT

AWARDED TO

DATE

SIGNATURE

envision®

BACKYARD GETAWAY

BACKYARD GETAWAY PROJECT

STUDENT

envision

BACKYARD GETAWAY

backyard getaway expo

envision

Component 1: Building Your Project Portfolio
Total Possible Portfolio Points: 79 out of 100 total possible for project

Requirements	Possible Points	Teacher Points	Average Points
Portfolio Section 1: Climate and Terrain Features			
1. Computer-Generated Climate and Terrain Features Table: Analyze the range of different climates and terrain features found in your state or country. List three to five climates and terrains that you would enjoy best for your backyard. Create a titled table using the computer showing the characteristics of each climate and terrain.	3		
2. Climate and Terrain Features Choices: Using your features table, highlight a specific climate and one or two terrain features that you will choose for your backyard. Explain your reasoning in making these choices.	2		
3. Physical Map: Create a physical map of your backyard. Your backyard can have any shape you like as long as it remains a total of one acre in size – no larger, no smaller. Find the conversion for an acre into square feet or square yards and include a scale with your map. Label the terrain features in your yard, keeping them to scale. Be sure to include a creative map title and a key. Refine this map as you progress through the upcoming objectives.	4		
4. Road Map: Create a road map of your backyard using the computer or a pencil and paper. Draw and label the area locations in your yard as you work on the upcoming objectives. Create a key with symbols if needed. Be sure to include your creative map title and map scale. Refine this map as needed.	4		
Portfolio Section 2: Area Locations			
1. Relaxation Area Reflection: Reflect on and make an unlimited list of activities and items that are relaxing to you. They may be activities such as reading, music, or exercise. They may be items such as foods, types of art, or animals. Look over your list. Record ways to incorporate them into your backyard relaxation area and explain why you chose them.	3		
2. Relaxation Area Diorama: Create a diorama of how your relaxation area will look. Include all of the activities and other items you chose in number one above. Be creative, detailed, colorful, and include labels.	5		
3. Recreation Area Brainstorm: Brainstorm recreational activities that you enjoy or would like to enjoy. Some activity examples are: volleyball, croquet, swimming, ice-skating, bug collecting, bird watching, or rock wall climbing. Record creative ways that you could incorporate two to five of them in your backyard recreation area.	3		
4. Recreation Area Safety Rules Signs: For each of your backyard recreational activities, design a safety rules sign. Each titled sign should list important rules for being safe and playing fair with each of your recreational activities.	5		

5. Water Habitat Watercolor: Research various types of water habitats and the ecosystems found within each. Choose the water habitat you would like to have in your backyard. Create a watercolor artwork of your water habitat. Be sure to include all plant and animal life in and around your water habitat.	5		
6. Water Habitat Food Chain: Choose a specific animal at the bottom or top of a food chain in your water habitat. Find or create pictures of the other animals in that food chain. Organize them into a visual food chain chart complete with arrows, labels, and a title.	5		
7. Water Cycle Poem: Use the computer to compose a poem about your water habitat and how it is affected by each phase of the water cycle. Give your poem a title. It may be written in any style you like.	5		
8. Flower or Food Garden T-Chart and Choice: Make a titled two-column t-chart with the headings "Flower Garden" and "Food Garden". Below each column title, list positive and negative aspects of having each. Based on your chart, choose whether you would like to have a flower garden or a food garden in your backyard. Explain your decision below the chart.	4		
9. Flower or Food Garden Flipbook: Step 1, Flower or Food Garden Page Set-Up: List at least ten flowers or foods you will grow in your garden. Record each plant's name on a blank sheet of paper. **Step 2, Flower or Food Garden Care:** Read about your garden plants and record important care information about each on its corresponding sheet of paper from Step 1. Be sure to locate information about maintenance, optimal soil conditions, spacing, planting depth, and amount of sunlight needed. Include your reference sources on each page. **Step 3, Flower or Food Garden Pictures:** Adhere a photo or illustration of each plant to the bottom of its respective page. **Step 4, Flipbook Assembly:** Organize your finished flower or food garden pages into a flipbook. Divide your pages into subgroups to create different sections in your flipbook. Include a table of contents. Make a creative cover for your book with a special name for your garden.	7		
10. Flower or Food Garden Interdependence Fictional Story: Research more plants or animals that might be found in your backyard. Write a fictional story that includes important story elements and incorporates the animals' interdependence. Be creative and title your story.	5		
11. State or Country Tribute Cards: Step 1, State or Country Tribute Area Research: Research any aspect of your state's or country's history that interests you. Take notes in your own words on the information you find. Be sure to reference your sources for the information you obtain. **Step 2, State or Country Tribute Subtopic Card Set-Up:** Organize your notes into four or more subtopics and give each subtopic a title. Record each subtopic title on the top line of a five-by-eight-inch index card. **Step 3, State or Country Tribute Paragraphs:** Using each set of subtopic notes, write at least one formal paragraph about each subtopic. Write each paragraph on the lines below the corresponding subtopic title on each index card you set up in Step 2. Be sure your paragraphs relate to the main state or country aspect you originally researched, and that they are written in your own words.	7		

12. State or Country Tribute Artworks: To accompany each of your state or country tribute writings, create a piece of art to display in your backyard state or country tribute area. One of your art pieces must be some type of sculpture. You may use any medium or combination of media you wish. Media might include: naturally found materials, recycled materials, household items, clay, or papier-mâché. Be creative and have fun with these artworks!	7		
Remaining Portfolio Materials			
1. Table of Contents: Write a table of contents that lists all the sections of your portfolio along with their corresponding page numbers.	2		
2. Cover Page: Create an eye-catching cover page for your portfolio that includes an original title for your project as well as your name and the Classroom Presentation date.	1		
3. Portfolio: Organize all of your materials in a three-ring binder. The table of contents should come first, followed by your work from Portfolio Sections 1 and 2 above in the order presented. Your cover page should go on the front of the portfolio.	2		
TOTAL PORTFOLIO POINTS	**79**		

Component 2: Creating Your Project Exhibit
Total Possible Exhibit Points: 15 out of 100 total possible for project

1. State or Country Tribute Mini Museum: Arrange your state or country tribute artworks with their written accompaniments to create a miniature museum within your exhibit.	2		
2. Backyard Getaway Model: Create a miniature model of your backyard. Label each area location from Portfolio Section 2 and make it as detailed and creative as possible.	7		
3. Display Board: Use a large two- or three-panel display board to create an "advertisement" for your Backyard Getaway. It must include your project's title and your name. You may then choose to add any of the required items or any additional materials that you wish.	3		
4. Exhibit: Arrange your portfolio, relaxation area diorama, flower or food garden flipbook, state or country mini museum, Backyard Getaway model, and any additional materials you wish to include in an appealing and informative way.	3		
TOTAL EXHIBIT POINTS	**15**		

TEACHER ASSESSMENT

Component 3: Giving Your Classroom Presentation
Total Possible Classroom Presentation Points: 6 out of 100 total possible for project

1. What to Include in Your Presentation:			
• Climate and Terrain Features Choices: Share your climate and terrain features choices. Explain your reasoning for making those choices.	1		
• Maps: Display your physical map and road map while explaining the features of each.	2		
• Area Highlights: Explain one component from each of your backyard areas, pointing to any relevant materials in your exhibit.	1		
• Portfolio: Show your portfolio and explain one component that you would like to highlight.	1		
• Mini Museum: Show and explain the components of your state or country mini museum.	1		
TOTAL CLASSROOM PRESENTATION POINTS	**6**		
TOTAL PROJECT POINTS	**100**		

STUDENT SELF-ASSESSMENT

Component 1: Building Your Project Portfolio
Total Possible Portfolio Points: 79 out of 100 total possible for project

Requirements	Possible Points	Student Points
Portfolio Section 1: Climate and Terrain Features		
1. Computer-Generated Climate and Terrain Features Table: Analyze the range of different climates and terrain features found in your state or country. List three to five climates and terrains that you would enjoy best for your backyard. Create a titled table using the computer showing the characteristics of each climate and terrain.	3	
2. Climate and Terrain Features Choices: Using your features table, highlight a specific climate and one or two terrain features that you will choose for your backyard. Explain your reasoning in making these choices.	2	
3. Physical Map: Create a physical map of your backyard. Your backyard can have any shape you like as long as it remains a total of one acre in size – no larger, no smaller. Find the conversion for an acre into square feet or square yards and include a scale with your map. Label the terrain features in your yard, keeping them to scale. Be sure to include a creative map title and a key. Refine this map as you progress through the upcoming objectives.	4	
4. Road Map: Create a road map of your backyard using the computer or a pencil and paper. Draw and label the area locations in your yard as you work on the upcoming objectives. Create a key with symbols if needed. Be sure to include your creative map title and map scale. Refine this map as needed.	4	
Portfolio Section 2: Area Locations		
1. Relaxation Area Reflection: Reflect on and make an unlimited list of activities and items that are relaxing to you. They may be activities such as reading, music, or exercise. They may be items such as foods, types of art, or animals. Look over your list. Record ways to incorporate them into your backyard relaxation area and explain why you chose them.	3	
2. Relaxation Area Diorama: Create a diorama of how your relaxation area will look. Include all of the activities and other items you chose in number one above. Be creative, detailed, colorful, and include labels.	5	
3. Recreation Area Brainstorm: Brainstorm recreational activities that you enjoy or would like to enjoy. Some activity examples are: volleyball, croquet, swimming, ice-skating, bug collecting, bird watching, or rock wall climbing. Record creative ways that you could incorporate two to five of them in your backyard recreation area.	3	
4. Recreation Area Safety Rules Signs: For each of your backyard recreational activities, design a safety rules sign. Each titled sign should list important rules for being safe and playing fair with each of your recreational activities.	5	

5. Water Habitat Watercolor: Research various types of water habitats and the ecosystems found within each. Choose the water habitat you would like to have in your backyard. Create a watercolor artwork of your water habitat. Be sure to include all plant and animal life in and around your water habitat.	5	
6. Water Habitat Food Chain: Choose a specific animal at the bottom or top of a food chain in your water habitat. Find or create pictures of the other animals in that food chain. Organize them into a visual food chain chart complete with arrows, labels, and a title.	5	
7. Water Cycle Poem: Use the computer to compose a poem about your water habitat and how it is affected by each phase of the water cycle. Give your poem a title. It may be written in any style you like.	5	
8. Flower or Food Garden T-Chart and Choice: Make a titled two-column t-chart with the headings "Flower Garden" and "Food Garden". Below each column title, list positive and negative aspects of having each. Based on your chart, choose whether you would like to have a flower garden or a food garden in your backyard. Explain your decision below the chart.	4	
9. Flower or Food Garden Flipbook: Step 1, Flower or Food Garden Page Set-Up: List at least ten flowers or foods you will grow in your garden. Record each plant's name on a blank sheet of paper. **Step 2, Flower or Food Garden Care:** Read about your garden plants and record important care information about each on its corresponding sheet of paper from Step 1. Be sure to locate information about maintenance, optimal soil conditions, spacing, planting depth, and amount of sunlight needed. Include your reference sources on each page. **Step 3, Flower or Food Garden Pictures:** Adhere a photo or illustration of each plant to the bottom of its respective page. **Step 4, Flipbook Assembly:** Organize your finished flower or food garden pages into a flipbook. Divide your pages into subgroups to create different sections in your flipbook. Include a table of contents. Make a creative cover for your book with a special name for your garden.	7	
10. Flower or Food Garden Interdependence Fictional Story: Research more plants or animals that might be found in your backyard. Write a fictional story that includes important story elements and incorporates the animals' interdependence. Be creative and title your story.	5	
11. State or Country Tribute Cards: Step 1, State or Country Tribute Area Research: Research any aspect of your state's or country's history that interests you. Take notes in your own words on the information you find. Be sure to reference your sources for the information you obtain. **Step 2, State or Country Tribute Subtopic Card Set-Up:** Organize your notes into four or more subtopics and give each subtopic a title. Record each subtopic title on the top line of a five-by-eight-inch index card. **Step 3, State or Country Tribute Paragraphs:** Using each set of subtopic notes, write at least one formal paragraph about each subtopic. Write each paragraph on the lines below the corresponding subtopic title on each index card you set up in Step 2. Be sure your paragraphs relate to the main state or country aspect you originally researched, and that they are written in your own words.	7	

12. State or Country Tribute Artworks: To accompany each of your state or country tribute writings, create a piece of art to display in your backyard state or country tribute area. One of your art pieces must be some type of sculpture. You may use any medium or combination of media you wish. Media might include: naturally found materials, recycled materials, household items, clay, or papier-mâché. Be creative and have fun with these artworks!	7	
Remaining Portfolio Materials		
1. Table of Contents: Write a table of contents that lists all the sections of your portfolio along with their corresponding page numbers.	2	
2. Cover Page: Create an eye-catching cover page for your portfolio that includes an original title for your project as well as your name and the Classroom Presentation date.	1	
3. Portfolio: Organize all of your materials in a three-ring binder. The table of contents should come first, followed by your work from Portfolio Sections 1 and 2 above in the order presented. Your cover page should go on the front of the portfolio.	2	
TOTAL PORTFOLIO POINTS	**79**	

Component 2: Creating Your Project Exhibit
Total Possible Exhibit Points: 15 out of 100 total possible for project

1. State or Country Tribute Mini Museum: Arrange your state or country tribute artworks with their written accompaniments to create a miniature museum within your exhibit.	2	
2. Backyard Getaway Model: Create a miniature model of your backyard. Label each area location from Portfolio Section 2 and make it as detailed and creative as possible.	7	
3. Display Board: Use a large two- or three-panel display board to create an "advertisement" for your Backyard Getaway. It must include your project's title and your name. You may then choose to add any of the required items or any additional materials that you wish.	3	
4. Exhibit: Arrange your portfolio, relaxation area diorama, flower or food garden flipbook, state or country mini museum, Backyard Getaway model, and any additional materials you wish to include in an appealing and informative way.	3	
TOTAL EXHIBIT POINTS	**15**	

STUDENT SELF-ASSESSMENT

Component 3: Giving Your Classroom Presentation
Total Possible Classroom Presentation Points: 6 out of 100 total possible for project

1. What to Include in Your Presentation:		
• Climate and Terrain Features Choices: Share your climate and terrain features choices. Explain your reasoning for making those choices.	1	
• Maps: Display your physical map and road map while explaining the features of each.	2	
• Area Highlights: Explain one component from each of your backyard areas, pointing to any relevant materials in your exhibit.	1	
• Portfolio: Show your portfolio and explain one component that you would like to highlight.	1	
• Mini Museum: Show and explain the components of your state or country mini museum.	1	
TOTAL CLASSROOM PRESENTATION POINTS	**6**	
TOTAL PROJECT POINTS	**100**	

EXAMPLE BACKYARD GETAWAY
STUDENT RESOURCE CARDS

envision®

An inspirational real-world program for gifted learners

Student Resources Cards

Melanie L. Bondy

GRADE 4

 ## COMPUTER-GENERATED CLIMATE AND TERRAIN FEATURES TABLE

An information table utilizes headings, columns, and rows to organize information. Tables help you to visualize information both across a row and down a column.

Organize your Climate and Terrain Features Table to display three to five climates and terrain features found in your state or country. Your table should be organized in a way that is understandable and easy to read. Label the different sections of the table correctly, and give it a title.

EXAMPLE

CLIMATE AND TERRAIN FEATURES OF MICHIGAN By Shanda		
MICHIGAN CLIMATES		
Average January Temperature	Average July Temperature	Average Yearly Precipitation
Below 10°F	Below 60°F	More than 35"
10 – 18°F	60 – 68°F	30 – 35"
18 – 22°F	68 – 75°F	23 – 30"
Above 22°F	Above 75°F	Less than 23"
MICHIGAN TERRAIN FEATURES		
Small Mountains; Beaches and Dunes; Forests with Small Hills; Small Lakes and Rivers		

 # CLIMATE AND TERRAIN FEATURES CHOICES

Now that you have created a table showing the various climates and terrain features in your state or country, you can use it to decide what your backyard climate will be and what terrain features it will have.

In your table, highlight a specific climate and one or two terrain features that you will choose for your backyard. Beneath your chart explain your reasons for making these choices.

EXAMPLE

CLIMATE AND TERRAIN FEATURES OF MICHIGAN By Shanda		
MICHIGAN CLIMATES		
Average January Temperature	Average July Temperature	Average Yearly Precipitation
Below 10°F	Below 60°F	More than 35"
10 – 18°F	60 – 68°F	30 – 35"
18 – 22°F	68 – 75°F	23 – 30"
Above 22°F	Above 75°F	Less than 23"
Michigan Terrain Features		
Small Mountains; Beaches and Dunes; Forests with Small Hills; Small Lakes and Rivers		

My backyard paradise will be cold but tolerable in the winter so that I can enjoy some outdoor...

PHYSICAL MAP

Physical maps show terrain such as rivers, ponds, hills, and mountains. They may or may not show actual elevations. Once you create your physical map, you can use it as a reference for making decisions about other aspects of your backyard.

When drawing your map you may want to use pencil or the computer in case you want to make adjustments to it while progressing through the remaining objectives. Another helpful technique is to use graph paper, or an image of graph paper if you are creating your map on the computer. Each square can represent a square unit of measure, which should make it easier to both create and read. Remember to include a scale, a key or labels, and a creative title.

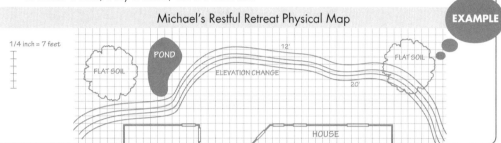

Michael's Restful Retreat Physical Map

EXAMPLE

ROAD MAP

A road map does not always show only roads. It can also show various points of interest in an area. Your backyard road map will be created as you progress through Component 2 of your Student Instruction Guide. Keep your map consistent with the way you created your physical map with regards to media and style so that it is easy to create and read.

Begin with an outline of your physical map. Draw and label the area locations in your backyard as you work on the Area Location objectives. Create a key with symbols if needed. Be sure to include your creative map title and map scale.

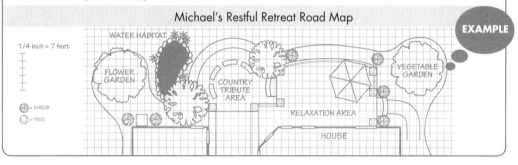

Michael's Restful Retreat Road Map

EXAMPLE

RELAXATION AREA DIORAMA

Dioramas are miniature models of a scene using three-dimensional objects placed in front of a background.

One container that is easy to use for a diorama is a box placed on its side. You can apply a background to the inside of the box that you have created separately. Your objects can also be made separately and then attached to the inside of the box. Some ideas for materials are: colored cardboard, fish line, thread, clay, glitter, colored plastic wrap, sand, buttons, and other household materials. Be creative, detailed, colorful, and include labels.

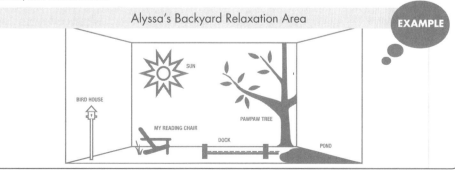

Alyssa's Backyard Relaxation Area

EXAMPLE

RECREATION AREA SAFETY RULES SIGNS

Signs with safety and fair play rules are important for keeping people safe while allowing them to have fun. A rule is a specific, expected way of behaving. For example, "Swim only with an adult present" is a rule you would probably see at a pool or lake.

Be sure to consider all important safety issues and fair play guidelines for each recreational activity in your backyard as you create your rules signs. List each sign's rules in order of importance. Be creative with the signs so people will want to read them.

ANDREW'S POOL SAFETY RULES

SWIM ONLY WITH AN ADULT PRESENT

ALWAYS WALK

NO DIVING IN SHALLOW AREA

ACTIVE FIRE PIT

CAUTION! HOT SURFACE

PLEASE EXTINGUISH WHEN NOT IN USE

Danger

EXAMPLES

WATER HABITAT FOOD CHAIN

A food chain depicts various animals within the same ecosystem and the ways in which they are connected by consumption.

Start by finding or creating a picture of a specific animal in your water habitat ecosystem. Next, find or create a picture of an animal that is either eaten by your first animal or eats your first animal. From there, find or create pictures of other animals that are eaten or eat the animals you already have until you have included all of the animals in that chain. Organize and mount the animal pictures onto paper to create your food chain. Remember to include arrows, labels, and a title.

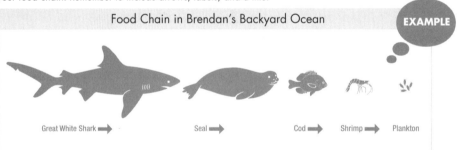

Food Chain in Brendan's Backyard Ocean

EXAMPLE

Great White Shark ➡   Seal ➡   Cod ➡ Shrimp ➡ Plankton

WATER CYCLE POEM

Poetry is an excellent way to express feelings and create imagery through creative writing. There are many different types of poetry including sonnets, haiku, and narrative poems. Poems usually use various literary devices such as metaphors, onomatopoeia, and symbolism. Often poems have some type of rhythmic quality, and they do not have to rhyme.

There are many different ways to approach poetry writing. Since your poem may be written in any style, your method for writing it will be up to you. It might be useful to read various poems before beginning yours. It can also be helpful to record various phrases separately before assembling them into a formal poem. You may even need to write more than one poem before deciding on your final version. Just make sure that the poem describes your water habitat and the ways in which it is affected by each phase of the water cycle.

Water Dance By Kristen

Waves dance along

Toss up their white sun-lit petticoats

Until dark clouds suddenly thunder in

Fiercely they flash their warning...

EXAMPLE

FLOWER OR FOOD GARDEN T-CHART AND CHOICE

A T-chart is a graphic organizer that is divided into two columns by lines that look like the letter T. T-charts are useful when you want to compare and contrast two choices.

Your T-chart will compare the positive and negative aspects of a flower garden and a food garden. Title your chart and list as many positive and negative aspects of each garden type that you can think of. Look over the lists for each type of garden and use them to evaluate which type of garden would be best for you. Remember to explain your decision below the chart.

EXAMPLE

POSITIVE AND NEGATIVE ASPECTS OF TWO GARDEN TYPES By Mitzi	
Flower Garden	**Food Garden**
Positive Aspects	Positive Aspects
Is eye-catching I could sell … I'd love to grow …	Will produce food I could try … I could make …
Negative Aspects	Negative Aspects
Have to … Some are …	Have to … Need to watch for …

I have decided that I will plant a food garden. I think it would be fun to have different sections within my garden for…

FLOWER OR FOOD GARDEN
INTERDEPENDENCE FICTIONAL STORY

Interdependence includes the many ways in which plants and animals adapt to their environments and rely on one another for energy and survival.

To create your story, research some more plants or animals that might be found in your backyard setting. Think creatively about how they might have a fictional relationship with one another. Incorporate important story elements such as: setting, plot, conflict, character, point of view, and theme. Also creatively incorporate how the animals are interdependent. Title your story.

EXAMPLE

AZUREUS THE MIGHTY BLUE FROG by Scott

Meet Azureus: a tiny blue poison dart frog who lives in my backyard. Azureus grew up in South America, deep in the dark moist parts of the jungle. His ancestors learned to survive in the jungle by eating insects that contained minute amounts of poison. As the frogs ate the insects, they would store the insect poison on their skin in case a snake, like Rudy the Red Tail, tried to eat them. It took only one flick of the tongue in the air for a would-be killer snake to sense the protective poison, then the frogs were safe. Over time, their once green skin turned bright blue. From then on predators like Rudy didn't even bother taking a whiff of them.

Now, Azureus' favorite lunchtime meal was a big pile of juicy beetle larvae, and it happened that on a particular Monday back in June, he spotted the best looking pile of larvae he had ever seen. Never one to let a meal go to waste, Azureus decided to dive right in. Little did he know…

TABLE OF CONTENTS

Your table of contents should be the first page in your portfolio, although you write it after you finish all of the pages inside. Writing it after finishing the contents allows you to be accurate with your page numbers and titles in case you make any last-minute changes. Your table of contents should list each section and the page it begins on. It should be neat and well organized, but feel free to be creative with your own layout.

EXAMPLE

TABLE OF CONTENTS

Page Number	Section Title
1	Computer-Generated Climate and Terrain Features Table
2	Climate and Terrain Features Choices
3	Physical Map
4	Road Map
5-6	Relaxation Area Reflection
7	Recreation Area Brainstorm

COVER PAGE

The cover page of your portfolio acts like the cover of a book. It should be eye-catching and should make someone want to open your portfolio to read about your project. It should include an original title for your project as well as your name and the Classroom Presentation date. Feel free to be creative and include artwork, design, and other creative touches.

FRONT COVER   SPINE   BACK COVER

EXAMPLE

PORTFOLIO

Your portfolio is what you will use to organize most of your paper items. A standard one- to one-and-a-half-inch binder with a clear plastic overlay works well. Arrange the contents of the portfolio in the order that they are mentioned in your Student Instruction Guide. The cover should include your name, Classroom Presentation date, and an original project title. You may wish to add tab dividers for each section listed in your table of contents, clear page protectors for each piece of paper, and creative personal touches.

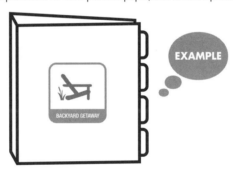

EXAMPLE

DISPLAY BOARD

The purpose of your display board is to draw attention to your project and to highlight some of its interesting information. It should be creative and colorful while remaining neat and well organized. Remember to make sure that it contains the necessary items listed on your Student Instruction Guide including your project's title and your name. The example below is to be used only as a guide; feel free to demonstrate your creativity. Tip: two- or three-panel display boards can be purchased at most craft stores. If you would rather make one, you can ask an adult to help construct one from a large cardboard box.

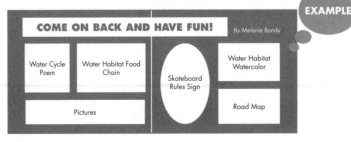

EXAMPLE

EXHIBIT

The purpose of your exhibit is to draw people's attention to your project. It should be neat, colorful, and creative. Your exhibit should include the items required in Component 2 of your Student Instruction Guide and any additional materials you wish to bring. The example below is to be used only as a guide; feel free to rearrange.

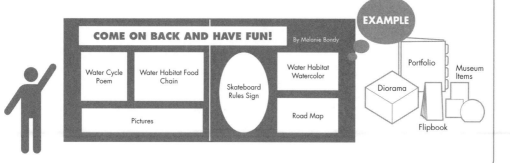

WHAT TO INCLUDE IN YOUR PRESENTATION

Your presentation will be a talk on what you learned, collected, and produced for your project. You should practice until you are comfortable with what you will say, but do not memorize a speech. Your presentation should be three to four minutes long and address the bulleted information listed in Component 3 your Student Instruction Guide.

REMEMBER TO:

- Take a deep breath, relax, and enjoy sharing.
- Greet your audience and introduce yourself.
- Speak clearly, loudly enough so everyone can hear you, and at a natural pace.
- Stand still and calm; don't fidget.
- Point to and show various visuals as you speak about them.
- Make eye contact with your audience, looking around the room naturally.
- Thank your audience when you are finished.

APPENDIX 2:
ENVIRONMENTAL DECLARATION
FORMS AND RESOURCE CARDS

Levels From Lowest to Highest:
KNOWLEDGE • COMPREHENSION • APPLICATION • ANALYSIS • EVALUATION • SYNTHESIS

Below you will find each Environmental Declaration requirement, along with its corresponding level of Bloom's Taxonomy.

> **IMPORTANT!**
>
> The levels listed above are cumulative. For example, the highest level of thinking, Synthesis, incorporates all other levels of thinking: Knowledge, Comprehension, Application, Analysis, and Evaluation.

COMPONENT 1

Building Your Project Portfolio
Total Possible Portfolio Points: 59 out of 100 total possible for project

Portfolio Section 1: Issue Information

1. Informational Notes (5 points): Learn about various environmental issues in your state and nation. **COMPREHENSION** Choose an issue with which you would most like to become involved. **EVALUATION** Read number two below before you begin so that you can organize and record your notes in a way that will help you complete that objective in an efficient manner. Gather and read as much information as you can about your issue through various media such as newspaper, television, radio, magazines, the Internet, or discussions. **COMPREHENSION** Take notes on all the information that you feel is important. Be sure to reference your sources for the information you obtain. **EVALUATION**

2. Special Terms Crossword Puzzle (5 points): As you read and learn information about your chosen environmental issue, create a list of glossary terms, their meanings, and the ways in which they relate to, or affect society. **COMPREHENSION** Organize this information into a crossword puzzle. Make a separate answer key for your puzzle, and give your puzzle a title. **SYNTHESIS**

3. Computer-Generated Line Graph (4 points): Using the computer, organize a set of important numerical data you discovered about your issue into a line graph. The data you choose should show changes over time. Include a key and give your graph a title. **SYNTHESIS**

4. Simple Actions Card (5 points): Evaluate various problems and solutions to the issue you are researching. Create a "top five" list of simple actions community members can take right now to help solve one or more of the problems. **EVALUATION** Design an easy-to-read three-by-five-inch card listing these actions. Include a heading that makes the reader aware of the issue. Make your card eye-catching so that if it was reproduced and distributed, people would want to read it. **SYNTHESIS**

5. Computer-Generated Mailing List (5 points): Evaluate who are, or could be the most influential people or organizations surrounding your environmental issue. **EVALUATION** Create a computer-generated mailing list with each person's or organization's contact information. Create subgroups within your mailing list such as: political leaders, community members, non-profit organizations, family members, state activists, or celebrities. **SYNTHESIS**

6. Solutions Choices (5 points): Research and explain how the main political parties of your country view your issue and its possible solutions. Analyze all of your gathered information and decide what your own solution ideas for this environmental issue will be. **EVALUATION**

Portfolio Section 2: Formal Persuasive Letter

1. Position Paragraph (4 points): Write a position paragraph with an attention-grabbing first sentence. Next, state your issue and some of the most common solution ideas you found. Lastly, state one or two of your official solution ideas for this issue. **COMPREHENSION**

2. Data Paragraph (4 points): Write a second paragraph that explains specifically cited data and explain how the data supports your solutions for the issue. **APPLICATION**

3. Core Value Paragraph (4 points): The third section of your letter must discuss at least one core democratic value and how it is affected by, or can be positively nurtured by your solutions to the issue. **APPLICATION**

4. Real-World Paragraph (4 points): Your letter's fourth section should describe real-world effects of your issue on society. Also discuss ways that your solutions will change your state and nation for the positive. **APPLICATION**

5. Restate Paragraph (4 points): The final paragraph of your letter should restate your issue and solutions. Conclude by directly appealing to the addressee. Your addressees will be the mailing list members created in Portfolio Section 1 above. Your appeal should be a request for the addressee to take specific action regarding one of your solutions. You might request political action, participation in a certain event, or simple actions on an individual level. **SYNTHESIS**

6. Formal Persuasive Letter (5 points): Add the correct business letter format to your paragraphs from above, keeping the paragraphs in order. Be sure that your request in the Restate Paragraph is appropriately worded for each person or organization on your mailing list. Send the appropriate letter to each member of your mailing list. **COMPREHENSION**

Remaining Portfolio Materials

1. Table of Contents (2 points): Write a table of contents that lists all the sections of your portfolio along with their corresponding page numbers. **COMPREHENSION**

2. Cover Page (1 point): Create an eye-catching cover page for your portfolio that includes an original title for your project as well as your name and the Classroom Presentation date. **SYNTHESIS**

3. Portfolio (2 points): Organize all of your materials in a three-ring binder. The table of contents should come first, followed by your work from Portfolio Sections 1 and 2 in the order presented. Your cover page should go on the front of the portfolio. **SYNTHESIS**

COMPONENT 2

Creating Your Project Exhibit

Total Possible Exhibit Points: 30 out of 100 total possible for project

1. Computer-Designed Bumper Sticker (4 points): Create a bumper sticker for your issue using the computer. Your sticker must contain an original self-designed symbol for your issue, and a positive catchy phrase that creates awareness for the issue. **SYNTHESIS**

2. "What's Right?" Illustration (5 points): Illustrate a scene depicting your environmental issue in real life. Include things that do and do not correctly follow your solution suggestions. Write directions for someone to locate and color the correct portions. Make a separate answer key either by listing descriptions of the correct portions or by making a photocopy of the original and coloring its correct portions. **SYNTHESIS**

3. Picture Cube (5 points): On each of six five-by-five-inch squares of paper, illustrate and label a specific core democratic value or aspect of society that will be positively affected in your state and nation if your environmental solutions are adopted. Attach your drawings to a self-made cube of cardstock or cardboard. Each side of your cube should measure five inches by five inches. **SYNTHESIS**

4. "Do's and Don'ts" Poster (5 points): Design a poster that teaches the most important "do's and don'ts" relating to your issue. It should have both words and graphics. Make it eye-catching so people will want to read it. **SYNTHESIS**

5. Visual Examples (5 points): Gather items to create at least three visual examples of how your environmental issue is either affected negatively or can be resolved positively. Label the items and include an explanation for each. **APPLICATION**

6. Display Board (3 points): Use a large two- or three-panel display board to create an "advertisement" for your Environmental Declaration. It must include your bumper sticker, your "What's right?" illustration, your project title, and your name. You may then choose to add any of the required items or any additional materials that you wish. **SYNTHESIS**

7. Exhibit (3 points): Arrange your portfolio, picture cube, "do's and don'ts" poster, visual examples, and any additional materials you wish to include in an appealing and informative way. **SYNTHESIS**

COMPONENT 3:

Giving Your Classroom Presentation

Total Possible Classroom Presentation Points: 11 out of 100 total possible for project

1. What to Include in Your Presentation:

• Documentary (10 points): Make a video recording, make a computer presentation, or write a script for a documentary that is directly connected to your environmental issue. It should be thorough, accurate, and well balanced. You may be creative with how you present the information, but you should speak in a serious tone and be well rehearsed. Title it and include citations and references for information sources. If it is a computer presentation or a written script, act as the documentary narrator and present it to your class as if you were being filmed. **SYNTHESIS**

2. Attire (1 point): Whether your presentation is recorded or live, dress in clothing that a documentary host might wear. **COMPREHENSION**

TEACHER COPY CHART

Step Number	Form Title	Number of Copies
1.1	Teacher Planning Guide	1 only
2.1-2.3	Parent Environmental Declaration Introduction Letter Student Environmental Declaration Introduction Letter Student Instruction Guide	1 completed, then 1 per student 1 completed only 1 only
3.1-3.4	Teacher Forms Checklist Student Commitment Contract	1 completed only 1 completed, then 1 per student
3.5	Student Environmental Declaration Introduction Letter* Student Instruction Guide* Environmental Declaration Resource Card Appendix Pages*	1 completed, then one per student 1 per student 1 per student (optional)
4.1-4.2	Student Checkpoint Organizer Teacher Checkpoint Record	1 per student 1 completed only
5.1-5.2	Student Expo Invitation	1 completed, then one per student
5.9-5.11	Student Certificate Student Name Sign (optional) Left Arrow Sign Right Arrow Sign	1 per student, then each completed 1 per student, then each completed Amount needed Amount needed
5.12-5.13	Teacher Assessment Student Self-Assessment	1 per student 1 per student

* Staple these items into a packet for each student

Events scheduled with the class are in black.

Week	Event (Step Numbers)	Day and Date	Time
1	Planning and Preparing for the Quarter (1.1-1.2)		
	Prep. for Environmental Declaration Introduction (2.1-2.3)		
	Environmental Declaration Introduction (2.4-2.7)		
	Prep. for Environmental Declaration Implementation (3.1-3.6)		
	Environmental Declaration Implementation (3.7-3.17)		
3	Preparation for the Checkpoint Meetings (4.1-4.2)		
	Distribute Checkpoint Organizers (4.3-4.6)		
	Checkpoint Meetings (4.7-4.12)		
5	Preparation for the Checkpoint Meetings (4.1-4.2)		
	Distribute Checkpoint Organizers (4.3-4.6)		
	Checkpoint Meetings (4.7-4.12)		
7	Preparation for the Checkpoint Meetings (4.1-4.2)		
	Distribute Checkpoint Organizers (4.3-4.6)		
	Checkpoint Meetings (4.7-4.12)		
8	Prep. for the Environmental Declaration Expo (5.1-5.2)		
	Invite Families to Environmental Declaration Expo (5.3-5.4)		
	Prep. for Environmental Declaration Expo Ctd. (5.5-5.11)		
9	Prep. for Classroom Presentations and the Environmental Declaration Expo (5.12-5.15)		
	Classroom Presentations (6A.1-6A.13 or 6B.1-6B.12)		
	Classroom Expo and Student Self-Assessment (7A.1-7A.9 or 7B.1-7B.10)		
10	Final Prep. for Environmental Declaration Expo (8.1-8.10)		
	Environmental Declaration Expo (9.1-9.4)		
	Conclusion and Teacher Assessment (10.1-10.8)		
	Student Review (10.9-10.10)		

ENVIRONMENTAL
DECLARATION

parent environmental declaration introduction letter

Dear Parent(s),

Welcome to Environmental Declaration, the second of four Envision projects that will challenge and inspire your child. Environmental Declaration is designed to create a deep awareness about a state or national environmental issue and to allow your child a voice in the matter. Your child will have the opportunity to research environmental issues and choose a specific issue on which to focus. To complete the project portfolio your child will create a crossword puzzle, a line graph, an actions card, a mailing list, a persuasive letter, a bumper sticker, and an illustration.

For the project exhibit your child will create a picture cube geared toward core democratic values, a "do's and don'ts" poster, and visual examples of environmental affects or solutions related to the chosen issue. Lastly, your child will give a brief formal presentation to the class and share a self-created documentary.

A Student Instruction Guide will be provided to guide your child, step by step, through this process. The Instruction Guide is a comprehensive list of project requirements and is designed to engage higher-level thinking. The guide also references helpful Resource Cards, that provide additional explanations, ideas, tips, and directions. There will be a set of these cards in our classroom to which your child may refer.

Environmental Declaration is designed to be worked on independently during class time, free time, and at home. By scheduling several Checkpoint Meeting dates throughout the quarter, I will be able to monitor each student's progress. On these dates, I will meet with each student to discuss accomplishments and plan goals for the next checkpoint. I will also address any difficulties students might be having.

Environmental Declaration will conclude with a Project Expo. The expo will be your child's opportunity to share his or her finished project with family, friends, and other guests. You will receive a detailed invitation to the Project Expo later in the quarter.

Dates to Remember:

Checkpoint 1: _____

Checkpoint 2: _____

Checkpoint 3: _____

Classroom Presentation: _____

Environmental Declaration Expo: _____ , _____

Sincerely,

_____

_____

ENVIRONMENTAL
DECLARATION

student environmental declaration introduction letter

Dear Student,

Welcome to Environmental Declaration, the second of four Envision Program projects. This project is an exercise in choosing an environmental issue that is important to you and in voicing your research-based opinions about it. It will be a personal voyage of discovery and an opportunity to explore an issue that affects our society.

To begin, you will research environmental issues and choose one on which to focus. You will then create a crossword puzzle, a line graph, an actions card, a mailing list, a persuasive letter, a bumper sticker, and an illustration. Environmental Declaration is divided into four components. The first component involves organizing your environmental research in a project portfolio. For the second component, you will create an exhibit that presents key information and aspects about your chosen environmental issue. The third component is a classroom presentation given to an audience of your peers. This presentation will allow you to share your environmental issue research and a self-created documentary. The fourth and final component is the project expo, at which you will share your completed project with family, friends, and invited guests.

You will work on Environmental Declaration throughout the school day, during your free time, and at home. Generally, you will be expected to work on your own. You will consult with me periodically at Checkpoint Meetings to discuss your progress and receive guidance. Between the checkpoints, feel free to discuss your project with other Envision students.

The attached Student Instruction Guide contains all the information you will need to complete the required Environmental Declaration Project successfully. The Instruction Guide will challenge you to be resourceful, organized, and to think at a higher level.

Dates to Remember:

Checkpoint 1: _____

Checkpoint 2: _____

Checkpoint 3: _____

Classroom Presentation: _____

Environmental Declaration Expo: _____ , _____

After reading this introduction, you are now ready to begin thinking about environmental issues and planning your declaration. Good luck and have fun!

Sincerely,

_____

_____

Building Your Project Portfolio • Creating Your Project Exhibit
Presenting Your Project • Attending the Expo

BE CREATIVE!

IMPORTANT!

Resource cards are denoted by an Environmental Declaration icon [icon]. When you see one of these icons, you will know that there is a corresponding resource card available that gives additional helpful information and examples. Also, be sure to visit www.mindvinepress.com, other trustworthy Internet sites, and library reference materials for helpful resources and examples.

COMPONENT 1

Building Your Project Portfolio Total Possible Portfolio Points: 59 out of 100 total possible for project

For this project, you will choose an environmental issue that is important to you, research it, and voice your opinions about it. Complete the numbered requirements below, in order, as they build upon one another and will guide you smoothly through this planning process.

Note: "Component 1: Building Your Environmental Declaration Portfolio" is separated into three sections: "Portfolio Section 1: Issue Information", "Portfolio Section 2: Formal Persuasive Letter", and "Portfolio Section 3: Remaining Portfolio Materials".

STUDENT INSTRUCTION GUIDE

Portfolio Section 1: Issue Information

1. Informational Notes (5 points): Learn about various environmental issues in your state and nation. Choose an issue with which you would most like to become involved. Read number two below before you begin so that you can organize and record your notes in a way that will help you complete that objective in an efficient manner. Gather and read as much information as you can about your issue through various media such as newspaper, television, radio, magazines, the Internet, or discussions. Take notes on all the information that you feel is important. Be sure to reference your sources for the information you obtain.

2. **Special Terms Crossword Puzzle** (5 points): As you read and learn information about your chosen environmental issue, create a list of glossary terms, their meanings, and the ways in which they relate to, or affect society. Organize this information into a crossword puzzle. Make a separate answer key for your puzzle, and give your puzzle a title.

3. **Computer-Generated Line Graph** (4 points): Using the computer, organize a set of important numerical data you discovered about your issue into a line graph. The data you choose should show changes over time. Include a key and give your graph a title.

4. **Simple Actions Card** (5 points): Evaluate various problems and solutions to the issue you are researching. Create a "top five" list of simple actions community members can take right now to help solve one or more of the problems. Design an easy-to-read three-by-five-inch card listing these actions. Include a heading that makes the reader aware of the issue. Make your card eye-catching so that if it was reproduced and distributed, people would want to read it.

5. **Computer-Generated Mailing List** (5 points): Evaluate who are, or could be the most influential people or organizations surrounding your environmental issue. Create a computer-generated mailing list with each person's or organization's contact information. Create subgroups within your mailing list such as: political leaders, community members, non-profit organizations, family members, state activists, or celebrities.

6. Solutions Choices (5 points): Research and explain how the main political parties of your country view your issue and its possible solutions. Analyze all of your gathered information and decide what your own solution ideas for this environmental issue will be.

Portfolio Section 2: Formal Persuasive Letter

Write a formal persuasive letter in business letter format to send to each of the people on your mailing list from Portfolio Section 1. Be sure to use your own voice in your writing by including your feelings or even humor.

1. Position Paragraph (4 points): Write a position paragraph with an attention-grabbing first sentence. Next, state your issue and some of the most common solution ideas you found. Lastly, state one or two of your official solution ideas for this issue.

2. Data Paragraph (4 points): Write a second paragraph that explains specifically cited data and explain how the data supports your solutions for the issue.

3. Core Value Paragraph (4 points): The third section of your letter must discuss at least one core democratic value and how it is affected by, or can be positively nurtured by your solutions to the issue.

4. Real-World Paragraph (4 points): Your letter's fourth section should describe real-world effects of your issue on society. Also discuss ways that your solutions will change your state and nation for the positive.

5. Restate Paragraph (4 points): The final paragraph of your letter should restate your issue and solutions. Conclude by directly appealing to the addressee. Your addressees will be the mailing list members created in Portfolio Section 1 above. Your appeal should be a request for the addressee to take specific action regarding one of your solutions. You might request political action, participation in a certain event, or simple actions on an individual level.

6. **Formal Persuasive Letter** (5 points): Add the correct business letter format to your paragraphs from above, keeping the paragraphs in order. Be sure that your request in the Restate Paragraph is appropriately worded for each person or organization on your mailing list. Send the appropriate letter to each member of your mailing list.

Remaining Portfolio Materials

1.  **Table of Contents** (2 points): Write a table of contents that lists all the sections of your portfolio along with their corresponding page numbers.

2. **Cover Page** (1 point): Create an eye-catching cover page for your portfolio that includes an original title for your project as well as your name and the Classroom Presentation date.

3. **Portfolio** (2 points): Organize all of your materials in a three-ring binder. The table of contents should come first, followed by your work from Portfolio Sections 1and 2 in the order presented. Your cover page should go on the front of the portfolio.

You have now completed Component 1 of the Environmental Declaration Project. By completing your portfolio, you have created an important resource that will help you work on Components 2 and 3. Though several worthy challenges lie ahead, you are now prepared to meet each of them, knowing that you have laid the necessary groundwork that will increase your chances for success. Good luck as you move on to creating your project exhibit items.

COMPONENT 2
Creating Your Environmental Declaration Exhibit
Total Possible Exhibit Points: 30 out of 100 total possible for project

Having chosen and researched an important environmental issue, it is now time to design and create an informative and appealing exhibit of your work. The items you complete will be viewed by your classmates on the day of your Classroom Presentation and also by everyone who attends the Environmental Declaration Expo at the end of the term. As always, put your best work into designing, creating, and integrating your exhibit items.

Note:
Keep in mind that each item is only one part of the overall exhibit. In other words, no single item has to say everything about your project. Decide upon a purpose for each item. Consider how best to arrange your exhibit for the greatest effect.

1. **Computer-Designed Bumper Sticker** (4 points): Create a bumper sticker for your issue using the computer. Your sticker must contain an original self-designed symbol for your issue, and a positive catchy phrase that creates awareness for the issue.

2. "What's Right?" Illustration (5 points): Illustrate a scene depicting your environmental issue in real life. Include things that do and do not correctly follow your solution suggestions. Write directions for someone to locate and color the correct portions. Make a separate answer key either by listing descriptions of the correct portions or by making a photocopy of the original and coloring its correct portions.

3. **Picture Cube** (5 points): On each of six five-by-five-inch squares of paper, illustrate and label a specific core democratic value or aspect of society that will be positively affected in your state and nation if your environmental solutions are adopted. Attach your drawings to a self-made cube of cardstock or cardboard. Each side of your cube should measure five inches by five inches.

4. "Do's and Don'ts" Poster (5 points): Design a poster that teaches the most important "do's and don'ts" relating to your issue. It should have both words and graphics. Make it eye-catching so people will want to read it.

5. Visual Examples (5 points): Gather items to create at least three visual examples of how your environmental issue is either affected negatively or can be resolved positively. Label the items and include an explanation for each.

6. **Display Board** (3 points): Use a large two- or three-panel display board to create an "advertisement" for your Environmental Declaration. It must include your bumper sticker, your "What's right?" illustration, your project title, and your name. You may then choose to add any of the required items or any additional materials that you wish.

7. **Exhibit** (3 points): Arrange your portfolio, picture cube, "do's and don'ts" poster, visual examples, and any additional materials you wish to include in an appealing and informative way.

You have now completed Component 2 of the Environmental Declaration Project, giving you an important exhibit that creatively displays the many aspects of your environmental issue. Now that you have finished your portfolio and exhibit, you are ready to prepare for your Classroom Presentation (Component 3), during which you will share your project with your peers and teacher.

COMPONENT 3:

Giving Your Classroom Presentation
Total Possible Classroom Presentation Points: 11 out of 100 total possible for project

Now that you have chosen, researched, and discovered solutions for your environmental issue it is time to share your information with others. The Classroom Presentation is an opportunity to formally present your research and solutions and to share your hard work with your classmates and teacher. Your portfolio and exhibit contain all the information you will need to prepare for the presentation, so relax and have fun.

1. **What to Include in Your Presentation:**

Documentary (10 points): Make a video recording, make a computer presentation, or write a script for a documentary that is directly connected to your environmental issue. It should be thorough, accurate, and well balanced. You may be creative with how you present the information, but you should speak in a serious tone and be well rehearsed. Title it and include citations and references for information sources. If it is a computer presentation or a written script, act as the documentary narrator and present it to your class as if you were being filmed.

> **Note:**
> Your presentation should last between 3-4 minutes and should be rehearsed, but not a memorized speech. If your documentary will be longer than 4 minutes, please let your teacher know in advance.

2. Attire (1 point): Whether your presentation is recorded or live, dress in clothing that a documentary host might wear.

Bring to the Classroom Presentation:
All of your exhibit items and anything extra that you would like to enhance your exhibit. Remember to dress in clothing that a documentary host might wear.

You are now finished with Components 1, 2, and 3 – all of the assessed portions of your project. The final component, Attending the Environmental Declaration Expo, provides a festive closure to the Environmental Declaration Project.

COMPONENT 4:

Attending the Environmental Declaration Expo (The expo does not involve any points.)

Now that you have completed your project and presented it to your peers, it is time to share your work with family and friends at the Environmental Declaration Expo. The expo is an event that recognizes and celebrates the hard work you have done on your Environmental Declaration Project. At the expo, you will set up and stand by your exhibit as invited guests walk around informally and view the projects. Guests may ask you friendly questions about your project as they visit your exhibit, so have fun sharing your Environmental Declaration with them.

Bring to the Expo: all of your exhibit items and anything extra that you think will enhance your exhibit.

CONGRATULATIONS ON YOUR COMPLETED ENVIRONMENTAL DECLARATION PROJECT!

TEACHER FORMS CHECKLIST

use this checklist to record forms submitted by the students

student name	student commitment contract	student checkpoint organizer 1	student checkpoint organizer 2	student checkpoint organizer 3	expo invitation response	
					number attending	special equip. needed
1.						
2.						
3.						
4.						
5.						
6.						
7.						
8.						
9.						
10.						
11.						
12.						
13.						
14.						
15.						
16.						
17.						
18.						
19.						
20.						
21.						
22.						
23.						
24.						
25.						

STUDENT COMMITMENT CONTRACT

expectations

project work time

I agree to:

- be responsible for following my Student Instruction Guide to do my work.
- keep track of all my project materials.
- work hard on Envision without disturbing others.
- save my unanswered questions until my teacher is free to talk.

checkpoint meetings

I will come prepared with:

- my Student Instruction Guide.
- my completed Student Checkpoint Organizer.
- all of my project materials.

important dates and times

Checkpoint 1: _____

Checkpoint 2: _____

Checkpoint 3: _____

Classroom Presentation: _____

Environmental Declaration Expo: _____

_____

signatures

I agree to:

- meet expectations on the dates listed above.
- complete each of the Environmental Declaration requirements to the best of my ability.
- bring my project work to school each day so that I can work on it during extra time.
- take my project work from school each night so that I can work on it at home.

I understand that the Envision Environmental Declaration Project is a special opportunity, and that if I do not meet the above expectations, I may be asked to return to normal classroom activities.

Student Signature: _____ Date: _____

Parent Signature: _____ Date: _____

Please return this contract by: _____

STUDENT CHECKPOINT ORGANIZER

Student Name: _____ Checkpoint Date: _____

Environmental Issue Choice: _____

directions

1. Using your Student Instruction Guide, check off any requirements that you have completed up to this point.

2. Bring the following items to the Checkpoint Meeting:

• your Student Instruction Guide.

• your completed Student Checkpoint Organizer.

• all of your project materials.

questions

1. Which requirements have you completed up to this point?

_____

_____

2. Is there anything you need help with?

_____

_____

3. Is there anything else about your project that you would like to discuss?

_____

_____

4. List at least three goals you expect to accomplish by the next checkpoint.

_____

_____

student name	environmental issue choice	checkpoint 1 notes	checkpoint 2 notes	checkpoint 3 notes
1.				
2.				
3.				
4.				
5.				
6.				
7.				
8.				
9.				
10.				

(ENVIRONMENTAL DECLARATION)

YOU'RE INVITED!

envision

EXPO INVITATION RESPONSE

Please fill out and return by: _____

Student Name: _____

Student Attending? ☐ Yes ☐ No

Number of Student Guests Attending: _____

Will your child need any special school equipment for the expo (i.e., computer or TV)? Please List: _____

_____

Thank you.

We look forward to seeing you at this special event!

PLEASE JOIN US FOR OUR ENVISION ENVIRONMENTAL DECLARATION EXPO!

Why? _____

Who? _____

Where? _____

When? _____

Remember to bring your camera!

CERTIFICATE OF ACHIEVEMENT

ENVIRONMENTAL
DECLARATION

AWARDED TO

_____

DATE

_____

SIGNATURE

envision

ENVIRONMENTAL DECLARATION PROJECT

STUDENT

envision

ENVIRONMENTAL DECLARATION

environmental declaration expo

envision®

environmental declaration expo

envision®

TEACHER ASSESSMENT

Requirements	Possible Points	Teacher Points	Average Points
Portfolio Section 1: Issue Information			
1. Informational Notes: Learn about various environmental issues in your state and nation. Choose an issue with which you would most like to become involved. Gather and read as much information as you can about your issue through various media such as newspaper, television, radio, magazines, the Internet, or discussions. Take notes on all the information that you feel is important. Be sure to reference your sources for the information you obtain.	5		
2. Special Terms Crossword Puzzle: As you read and learn information about your chosen environmental issue, create a list of glossary terms, their meanings, and the ways in which they relate to, or affect society. Organize this information into a crossword puzzle. Make a separate answer key for your puzzle, and give your puzzle a title.	5		
3. Computer-Generated Line Graph: Using the computer, organize a set of important numerical data you discovered about your issue into a line graph. The data you choose should show changes over time. Include a key and give your graph a title.	4		
4. Simple Actions Card: Evaluate various problems and solutions to the issue you are researching. Create a "top five" list of simple actions community members can take right now to help solve one or more of the problems. Design an easy-to-read three-by-five-inch card listing these actions. Include a heading that makes the reader aware of the issue. Make your card eye-catching so that if it was reproduced and distributed, people would want to read it.	5		
5. Computer-Generated Mailing List: Evaluate who are, or could be the most influential people or organizations surrounding your environmental issue. Create a computer-generated mailing list with each person's or organization's contact information. Create subgroups within your mailing list such as: political leaders, community members, non-profit organizations, family members, state activists, or celebrities.	5		
6. Solutions Choices: Research and explain how the main political parties of your country view your issue and its possible solutions. Analyze all of your gathered information and decide what your own solution ideas for this environmental issue will be.	5		
Portfolio Section 2: Formal Persuasive Letter			
1. Position Paragraph: Write a position paragraph with an attention-grabbing first sentence. Next, state your issue and some of the most common solution ideas you found. Lastly, state one or two of your official solution ideas for this issue.	4		
2. Data Paragraph: Write a second paragraph that explains specifically cited data and explain how the data supports your solutions for the issue.	4		

3. Core Value Paragraph: The third section of your letter must discuss at least one core democratic value and how it is affected by, or can be positively nurtured by your solutions to the issue.	4		
4. Real-World Paragraph: Your letter's fourth section should describe real-world effects of your issue on society. Also discuss ways that your solutions will change your state and nation for the positive.	4		
5. Restate Paragraph: The final paragraph of your letter should restate your issue and solutions. Conclude by directly appealing to the addressee. Your addressees will be the mailing list members created in Portfolio Section 1 above. Your appeal should be a request for the addressee to take specific action regarding one of your solutions. You might request political action, participation in a certain event, or simple actions on an individual level.	4		
6. Formal Persuasive Letter: Add the correct business letter format to your paragraphs from above, keeping the paragraphs in order. Be sure that your request in the Restate Paragraph is appropriately worded for each person or organization on your mailing list. Send the appropriate letter to each member of your mailing list.	5		
Remaining Portfolio Materials			
1. Table of Contents: Write a table of contents that lists all the sections of your portfolio along with their corresponding page numbers.	2		
2. Cover Page: Create an eye-catching cover page for your portfolio that includes an original title for your project as well as your name and the Classroom Presentation date.	1		
3. Portfolio: Organize all of your materials in a three-ring binder. The table of contents should come first, followed by your work from Portfolio Sections 1 and 2 in the order presented. Your cover page should go on the front of the portfolio.	2		
TOTAL PORTFOLIO POINTS	**59**		

Component 2: Creating Your Environmental Declaration Exhibit
Total Possible Exhibit Points: 30 out of 100 total possible for project

1. Computer-Designed Bumper Sticker: Create a bumper sticker for your issue using the computer. Your sticker must contain an original self-designed symbol for your issue, and a positive catchy phrase that creates awareness for the issue.	4		
2. "What's Right?" Illustration: Illustrate a scene depicting your environmental issue in real life. Include things that do and do not correctly follow your solution suggestions. Write directions for someone to locate and color the correct portions. Make a separate answer key either by listing descriptions of the correct portions or by making a photocopy of the original and coloring its correct portions.	5		

3. Picture Cube: On each of six five-by-five-inch squares of paper, illustrate and label a specific core democratic value or aspect of society that will be positively affected in your state and nation if your environmental solutions are adopted. Attach your drawings to a self-made cube of cardstock or cardboard. Each side of your cube should measure five inches by five inches.	5		
4. "Do's and Don'ts" Poster: Design a poster that teaches the most important "do's and don'ts" relating to your issue. It should have both words and graphics. Make it eye-catching so people will want to read it.	5		
5. Visual Examples: Gather items to create at least three visual examples of how your environmental issue is either affected negatively or can be resolved positively. Label the items and include an explanation for each.	5		
6. Display Board: Use a large two- or three-panel display board to create an "advertisement" for your Environmental Declaration. It must include your bumper sticker, your "What's right?" illustration, your project title, and your name. You may then choose to add any of the required items or any additional materials that you wish.	3		
7. Exhibit: Arrange your portfolio, picture cube, "do's and don'ts" poster, visual examples, and any additional materials you wish to include in an appealing and informative way.	3		
TOTAL EXHIBIT POINTS	**30**		

Component 3: Giving Your Classroom Presentation
Total Possible Classroom Presentation Points: 11 out of 100 total possible for project

1. What to Include in Your Presentation: • Documentary: Make a video recording, make a computer presentation, or write a script for a documentary that is directly connected to your environmental issue. It should be thorough, accurate, and well balanced. You may be creative with how you present the information, but you should speak in a serious tone and be well rehearsed. Title it and include citations and references for information sources. If it is a computer presentation or a written script, act as the documentary narrator and present it to your class as if you were being filmed.	10		
2. Attire: Whether your presentation is recorded or live, dress in clothing that a documentary host might wear.	1		
TOTAL CLASSROOM PRESENTATION POINTS	**11**		
TOTAL PROJECT POINTS	**100**		

STUDENT SELF-ASSESSMENT

Component 1: Building Your Project Portfolio
Total Possible Portfolio Points: 59 out of 100 total possible for project

Requirements	Possible Points	Student Points
Portfolio Section 1: Issue Information		
1. Informational Notes: Learn about various environmental issues in your state and nation. Choose an issue with which you would most like to become involved. Gather and read as much information as you can about your issue through various media such as newspaper, television, radio, magazines, the Internet, or discussions. Take notes on all the information that you feel is important. Be sure to reference your sources for the information you obtain.	5	
2. Special Terms Crossword Puzzle: As you read and learn information about your chosen environmental issue, create a list of glossary terms, their meanings, and the ways in which they relate to, or affect society. Organize this information into a crossword puzzle. Make a separate answer key for your puzzle, and give your puzzle a title.	5	
3. Computer-Generated Line Graph: Using the computer, organize a set of important numerical data you discovered about your issue into a line graph. The data you choose should show changes over time. Include a key and give your graph a title.	4	
4. Simple Actions Card: Evaluate various problems and solutions to the issue you are researching. Create a "top five" list of simple actions community members can take right now to help solve one or more of the problems. Design an easy-to-read three-by-five-inch card listing these actions. Include a heading that makes the reader aware of the issue. Make your card eye-catching so that if it was reproduced and distributed, people would want to read it.	5	
5. Computer-Generated Mailing List: Evaluate who are, or could be the most influential people or organizations surrounding your environmental issue. Create a computer-generated mailing list with each person's or organization's contact information. Create subgroups within your mailing list such as: political leaders, community members, non-profit organizations, family members, state activists, or celebrities.	5	
6. Solutions Choices: Research and explain how the main political parties of your country view your issue and its possible solutions. Analyze all of your gathered information and decide what your own solution ideas for this environmental issue will be.	5	
Portfolio Section 2: Formal Persuasive Letter		
1. Position Paragraph: Write a position paragraph with an attention-grabbing first sentence. Next, state your issue and some of the most common solution ideas you found. Lastly, state one or two of your official solution ideas for this issue.	4	
2. Data Paragraph: Write a second paragraph that explains specifically cited data and explain how the data supports your solutions for the issue.	4	

3. Core Value Paragraph: The third section of your letter must discuss at least one core democratic value and how it is affected by, or can be positively nurtured by your solutions to the issue.	4	
4. Real-World Paragraph: Your letter's fourth section should describe real-world effects of your issue on society. Also discuss ways that your solutions will change your state and nation for the positive.	4	
5. Restate Paragraph: The final paragraph of your letter should restate your issue and solutions. Conclude by directly appealing to the addressee. Your addressees will be the mailing list members created in Portfolio Section 1 above. Your appeal should be a request for the addressee to take specific action regarding one of your solutions. You might request political action, participation in a certain event, or simple actions on an individual level.	4	
6. Formal Persuasive Letter: Add the correct business letter format to your paragraphs from above, keeping the paragraphs in order. Be sure that your request in the Restate Paragraph is appropriately worded for each person or organization on your mailing list. Send the appropriate letter to each member of your mailing list.	5	

Remaining Portfolio Materials

1. Table of Contents: Write a table of contents that lists all the sections of your portfolio along with their corresponding page numbers.	2	
2. Cover Page: Create an eye-catching cover page for your portfolio that includes an original title for your project as well as your name and the Classroom Presentation date.	1	
3. Portfolio: Organize all of your materials in a three-ring binder. The table of contents should come first, followed by your work from Portfolio Sections 1 and 2 in the order presented. Your cover page should go on the front of the portfolio.	2	
TOTAL PORTFOLIO POINTS	**59**	

Component 2: Creating Your Environmental Declaration Exhibit
Total Possible Exhibit Points: 30 out of 100 total possible for project

1. Computer-Designed Bumper Sticker: Create a bumper sticker for your issue using the computer. Your sticker must contain an original self-designed symbol for your issue, and a positive catchy phrase that creates awareness for the issue.	4	
2. "What's Right?" Illustration: Illustrate a scene depicting your environmental issue in real life. Include things that do and do not correctly follow your solution suggestions. Write directions for someone to locate and color the correct portions. Make a separate answer key either by listing descriptions of the correct portions or by making a photocopy of the original and coloring its correct portions.	5	

3. Picture Cube: On each of six five-by-five-inch squares of paper, illustrate and label a specific core democratic value or aspect of society that will be positively affected in your state and nation if your environmental solutions are adopted. Attach your drawings to a self-made cube of cardstock or cardboard. Each side of your cube should measure five inches by five inches.	5	
4. "Do's and Don'ts" Poster: Design a poster that teaches the most important "do's and don'ts" relating to your issue. It should have both words and graphics. Make it eye-catching so people will want to read it.	5	
5. Visual Examples: Gather items to create at least three visual examples of how your environmental issue is either affected negatively or can be resolved positively. Label the items and include an explanation for each.	5	
6. Display Board: Use a large two- or three-panel display board to create an "advertisement" for your Environmental Declaration. It must include your bumper sticker, your "What's right?" illustration, your project title, and your name. You may then choose to add any of the required items or any additional materials that you wish.	3	
7. Exhibit: Arrange your portfolio, picture cube, "do's and don'ts" poster, visual examples, and any additional materials you wish to include in an appealing and informative way.	3	
TOTAL EXHIBIT POINTS	**30**	

Component 3: Giving Your Classroom Presentation
Total Possible Classroom Presentation Points: 11 out of 100 total possible for project

1. What to Include in Your Presentation: • Documentary: Make a video recording, make a computer presentation, or write a script for a documentary that is directly connected to your environmental issue. It should be thorough, accurate, and well balanced. You may be creative with how you present the information, but you should speak in a serious tone and be well rehearsed. Title it and include citations and references for information sources. If it is a computer presentation or a written script, act as the documentary narrator and present it to your class as if you were being filmed.	10	
2. Attire: Whether your presentation is recorded or live, dress in clothing that a documentary host might wear.	1	
TOTAL CLASSROOM PRESENTATION POINTS	**11**	
TOTAL PROJECT POINTS	**100**	

EXAMPLE
ENVIRONMENTAL DECLARATION
STUDENT RESOURCE CARDS

SPECIAL TERMS CROSSWORD PUZZLE

Crossword puzzles are fun tools to teach, learn, and review information. They are often found in newspapers or puzzle books and are a very popular pastime for many people.

To begin your crossword puzzle, create the answer key. Write your special terms vertically or horizontally onto graph paper or on a computer grid so that one letter of each word fits in a single box. Color the unused squares. Next, number the beginning letter of each term in order, progressing from top to bottom and left to right. Some terms may share a number. Third, use the definitions and other information you collected to invent a clue for each term. Number each clue to correspond with the number of the box containing the first letter of the term in the puzzle. You will need to separate the clues into two groups: "Across" (horizontal) and "Down" (vertical). Finally, add a catchy title to your puzzle.

EXAMPLE

Have You Kissed a Manatee Today?
An Endangered Animal Crossword by Marilyn
Across:
    1) Mistaken for long ago
    4) A fragile...
    5) The smallest...

Down:
    1) Also called a blubbery blimp
    2) Type of animal...
    3) Frozen form...

Have You Kissed
a Manatee Today?
Answer Key
Across:
1) Mermaids
4) Egg
5) Atoms
Down:
1) Mermaids
2) Mammal
3) Ice

COMPUTER-GENERATED LINE GRAPH

Line graphs are an excellent way to display a set of data that has changed over a period of time. Plotted data points are connected to form a line, which allows patterns, trends, or unusual results to be seen.

To create your line graph, start by recording the time increments along the bottom or horizontal axis of the graph. On the vertical axis, up the left side of the graph, list your other incremental data points. Next, record a dot for each data amount above its corresponding time period. Connect the dots to form a line, include a graph title, and create a key or legend.

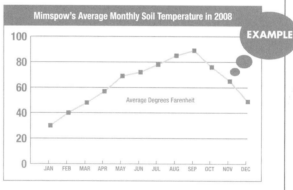

EXAMPLE

SIMPLE ACTIONS CARD

Creating awareness and giving people simple solutions are very important actions you can take when trying to help solve a community problem. One thing that people sometimes do is distribute small cards with simple solutions written on them. The cards are easy for people to read at a glance, and can be posted in a reminder place without taking up much space.

Once you come up with your top five list of simple actions, create a catchy heading that draws attention to your issue. Record it at the top of the card. Next, write your simple action suggestions in the most concise understandable way possible. Number and record them on the card below your title. Lastly, remember to make your card attractive.

EXAMPLE

COMPUTER-GENERATED MAILING LIST

A collection of names and contact information is often created and saved into a mailing list. These mailing lists, which are often organized into secondary or sub-groups, are useful when you want to send certain information to a number of people.

When you create your mailing list, be sure to organize your list into sub-groups and include each person's or organization's name, address, phone number, and email address. You may also want to jot a note with each entry that describes its relevance to your issue.

Influential People and Organizations for Air Quality

Community Members:

Mr. Larry Simon Smee
1007 Lakeshore Drive
Sunnyville, AL 20061
Business Phone: 818.252.9000
Email: Smee@cleancleanair.org
Influential clean air businessman.

Ms. Penelope R. Foster-Griver
2996 Beachwood Lane
Tree City, UT 41223
Home Phone: 221.453.8079
Email: hockeymom1@feefoo.com
Mother of three; active in clean air issues.

EXAMPLE

FORMAL PERSUASIVE LETTER

The purpose of a persuasive letter is to try to convince people to act or believe in a certain way. It should be thorough, convincing, and direct. It should also be typed in a business font such as Times New Roman and should have a character size of ten or twelve. The following example shows how to organize the beginning and ending of a letter in business format.

EXAMPLE

Your Name
Date
Your Address
Your Phone Number

Full Name of Addressee
Title of Addressee
Address of Company

Dear Mr. Bondy,

Are you…

In the year…

Sincerely,

(Your Signature)

Your Name

TABLE OF CONTENTS

Your table of contents should be the first page in your portfolio, although you write it after you finish all of the pages inside. Writing it after finishing the contents allows you to be accurate with your page numbers and titles in case you make any last-minute changes. Your table of contents should list each section and the page it begins on. It should be neat and well organized, but feel free to be creative with your own layout.

EXAMPLE

TABLE OF CONTENTS

COVER PAGE

The cover page of your portfolio acts like the cover of a book. It should be eye-catching and should make someone want to open your portfolio to read about your project. It should include an original title for your project as well as your name and the Classroom Presentation date. Feel free to be creative and include artwork, design, and other creative touches.

FRONT COVER   SPINE   BACK COVER

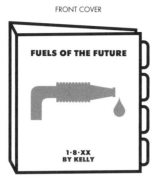

FUELS OF THE FUTURE

1·8·XX
BY KELLY

FUELS OF THE FUTURE

WILL YOU MAKE THE RIGHT CHOICE?

EXAMPLE

PORTFOLIO

Your portfolio is what you will use to organize most of your paper items. A standard one- to one-and-a-half-inch binder with a clear plastic overlay works well. Arrange the contents of the portfolio in the order that they are mentioned in your Student Instruction Guide. The cover should include your name, Classroom Presentation date, and an original project title. You may wish to add tab dividers for each section listed in your table of contents, clear page protectors for each piece of paper, and creative personal touches.

EXAMPLE

COMPUTER-DESIGNED BUMPER STICKER

Bumper stickers were originally created to attach to the bumpers of automobiles. Now they are so popular that people often attach them to other objects and even collect them.

Create your bumper sticker by formatting your document size to eleven inches by three inches and orienting it in the landscape, or horizontal position. Using your computer program's drawing tools, design a symbol for your issue and add a positive, catchy phrase that creates awareness for your issue.

EXAMPLE

HAVE YOU HUGGED A TREE TODAY?

PICTURE CUBE

Picture cubes are fun, eye-catching ways to display images or information. They can be any size and can be made out of a range of materials.

To begin yours, draw six five-by-five inch squares on a sheet of paper. On each square, illustrate and label a specific core democratic value or aspect of society that will be positively affected in your state or nation if your environmental solutions are adopted. Next, design a pattern on cardboard for a cube that measures five inches by five inches on each side. Cut out your pattern and form it into a cube. Lastly, cut out and attach your illustrations to the cube. Below is one pattern idea, but feel free to create your cube using any method you choose.

TIP: Make tabs to glue your box together.

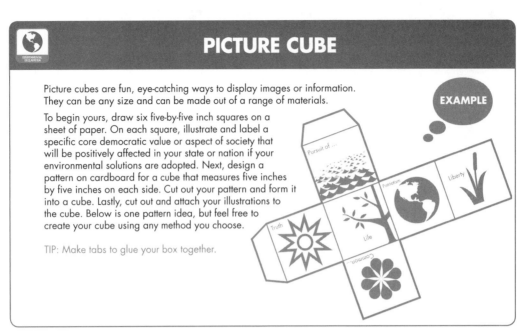

DISPLAY BOARD

The purpose of your display board is to draw attention to your project and to highlight some of its interesting information. It should be creative and colorful while remaining neat and well organized. Remember to make sure that it contains the necessary items listed on your Student Instruction Guide including your project's title and your name. The example below is to be used only as a guide; feel free to demonstrate your creativity. Tip: two- or three-panel display boards can be purchased at most craft stores. If you would rather make one, you can ask an adult to help construct one from a large cardboard box.

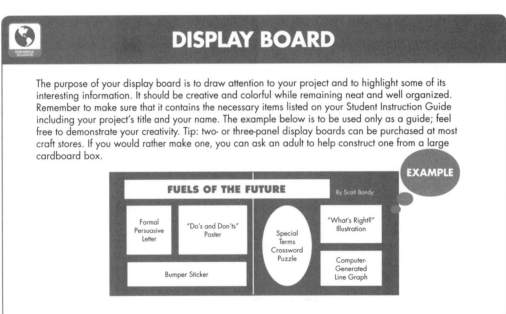

EXHIBIT

The purpose of your exhibit is to draw people's attention to your project. It should be neat, colorful, and creative. Your exhibit should include the items required in Component 2 of your Student Instruction Guide and any additional materials you wish to bring. The example below is to be used only as a guide; feel free to rearrange.

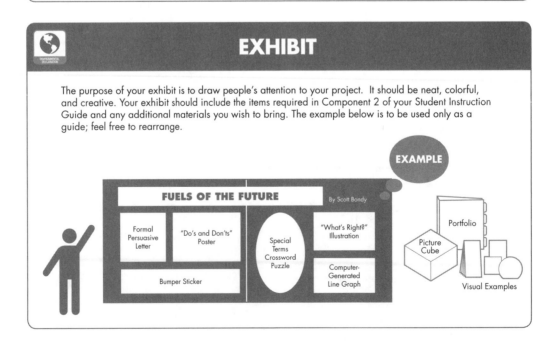

Your presentation will be a formal documentary on what you learned about your environmental issue. Whether you are filming it or presenting it live, you should practice until you are comfortable with what you will say, but do not memorize a speech. Your presentation should be three to four minutes long and address the bulleted information listed in Component 3 your Student Instruction Guide.

REMEMBER TO:

- Take a deep breath, relax, and enjoy sharing.
- Greet your audience and introduce yourself.
- Speak clearly, loudly enough so everyone can hear you, and at a natural pace.
- Stand still and calm; don't fidget.
- Point to and show various visuals as you speak about them.
- Make eye contact with your audience, looking around the room naturally.
- Thank your audience when you are finished.

 # DOCUMENTARY

A documentary is a non-fiction account of an event or topic usually presented in a serious tone. Documentaries are factually accurate and in-depth. Sometimes opinions and conflicting evidence are shared, especially if the topic is controversial or unresolved. If this is the case, the producer typically provides a balance of information about several aspects or viewpoints of the issue so that viewers can draw their own conclusions.

When you create your documentary, try to organize your informational notes into groups based on certain aspects or differing viewpoints of the issue. Use each group of notes to write a segment of your documentary's script, adding visuals whenever possible. Whether you video record your documentary or present it live, your script and use of visuals should be well rehearsed so that the presentation flows smoothly.

APPENDIX 3:
CIVIC MISSION FORMS AND
RESOURCE CARDS

Levels From Lowest to Highest:
KNOWLEDGE • COMPREHENSION • APPLICATION • ANALYSIS • EVALUATION • SYNTHESIS

Below you will find each Civic Mission requirement, along with its corresponding level of Bloom's Taxonomy.

> **IMPORTANT!**
> The levels listed above are cumulative. For example, the highest level of thinking, Synthesis, incorporates all other levels of thinking: Knowledge, Comprehension, Application, Analysis, and Evaluation.

COMPONENT 1
Building Your Project Portfolio
Total Possible Portfolio Points: 86 out of 100 total possible for project

Portfolio Section 1: Pre Civic Mission Event

1. Personal Interests and Talents Profile (5 points): Using the computer, create a list of activities that you enjoy or at which you excel. **EVALUATION** Your list may include anything you do recreationally, academically, or socially. Use the copy, cut, and paste tools to rearrange your list so that the activities you enjoy most and at which you succeed most are at the top of your list. Your list should then progress in order downward to the activities you like less or at which you are not as successful. **SYNTHESIS**

2. Academic Goal (4 points): Record a specific academic goal that you would like to accomplish through your Civic Mission project. It can be something completely new to you or a skill you would like to refine, but it must be academically based and measurable. Explain why you chose this goal. **EVALUATION**

3. Community Locality Ranking (4 points): Research community localities that fit your top interests and talents, could help accomplish your academic goal, and accept volunteer assistance. Rank them in order of those you would most like to serve. **EVALUATION**

4. Partnership Commitment (5 points): Beginning with your top-ranked locality choice, contact the person in charge of working with volunteers. Explain that you would like to assist with the locality's needs, and ask if you can work together to create a service-learning project that will benefit you both. Continue this process until you have a firm commitment from someone who will work with you. Highlight this locality on your list from number three above. **APPLICATION**

5. Service Need and Solution (5 points): Discuss your chosen locality's genuine needs with its contact person. Brainstorm solutions to the locality's various needs and write them down. **APPLICATION** Together choose and highlight one need and solution that you can realistically help with, that fits your time frame and your interests or talents, and that helps you reach your academic goal. Be sure that your contact person knows you will be doing most of the planning and legwork for this project. Also be sure to discuss and obtain permission for this solution with your parent before officially committing to the idea. **EVALUATION**

6. Service Action Plan (7 points): Carefully plan all of the steps you will need to take to prepare for, carry out, and complete your Civic Mission event. Plan your event with enough time to complete the Post Civic Mission Event objectives in Portfolio Section 3 below. Before proceeding, review your plans with the contact person at your locality to be sure that your plans will work. Also double-check everything with your parent. You may then proceed with implementing your plan. **SYNTHESIS**

7. Computer-Generated Reflection Journal (7 points): Using the computer, begin writing a Civic Mission reflection journal. Two to three times each week, reflect on what is happening in this process. Include your predictions, feelings, evaluations, progress on your academic goal, learning, and whatever else you would like. You may choose to add illustrations, photos, and mementos as well. **SYNTHESIS**

8. Computer-Designed T-Shirt (5 points): Using the computer, design a t-shirt that relates to your Civic Mission project and that you and other volunteers might wear. Your design should include both an original artistic aspect as well as a written message. **SYNTHESIS**

Portfolio Section 2: Civic Mission Event

1. Final Preparations (5 points): Double-check on any final preparations you need to complete before your Civic Mission event takes place. Confirm the final plans with your contact person. Discuss any safety procedures that you need to be aware of with your contact person. Also ask if there are any situations that you might need to be sensitive to while you work. Write any important or helpful information on a sheet of paper and include it with your service action plan. **COMPREHENSION**

2. Event Participation (8 points): With parent permission and supervision, participate in your chosen Civic Mission event. Follow your plan and do the best you can to help your community while accomplishing your goals. Enjoy yourself, take photos if you can, and try to go out of your comfort zone by doing things you might not normally do. **SYNTHESIS**

Portfolio Section 3: Post Civic Mission Event

1. Post-Event Reflection (8 points): In your reflection journal, write an in-depth entry about your Civic Mission event. Be sure to answer the following questions:

- How did your event strengthen your community and contribute to the common good? **APPLICATION**

- What types of personal growth took place for you? **APPLICATION**

- What did you learn about yourself, others, and the locality? **APPLICATION**

- Were your goals accomplished? Please explain. **EVALUATION**

- What special or unexpected events took place? **ANALYSIS**

- Did you enjoy planning and participating in this event? Why or why not? **EVALUATION**

- What should you have done differently? **EVALUATION**

- Would you participate in future service-learning events? Give your reasoning. **EVALUATION**

2. Creative Thank-You Card (5 points): Create a thank-you card for your community contact and the locality you served. Design the card so it is reflective of the event. Take photos of the card to include in your portfolio then send it, or wait to send it until after your project assessments have been completed. **SYNTHESIS**

3. Mobile of Learning (5 points): Design and create an artistic mobile showing various aspects of learning that took place for you with specific regards to your academic goal. Create a title and label each artistic element. **SYNTHESIS**

4. Personal Challenge Essay (4 points): Record a personal challenge you faced during this process and how you met that challenge. **EVALUATION**

5. Inspirational Message (4 points): Write about a moment that you will remember from this experience. Explain how that experience was meaningful to you in a way that might inspire others to become involved in service learning. **APPLICATION**

Remaining Portfolio Materials

1. Table of Contents (2 points): Write a table of contents that lists all the sections of your portfolio along with their corresponding page numbers. **COMPREHENSION**

2. Cover Page (1 point): Create an eye-catching cover page for your portfolio that includes an original title for your project as well as your name and the Classroom Presentation date. **SYNTHESIS**

3. Portfolio (2 points): Organize all of your materials in a three-ring binder. The table of contents should come first, followed by your work from Portfolio Sections 1, 2, and 3 above in the order presented. Your cover page should go on the front of the portfolio. **SYNTHESIS**

COMPONENT 2
Creating Your Project Exhibit

Total Possible Exhibit Points: 6 out of 100 total possible for project

1. Display Board (3 points): Use a large two- or three-panel display board to create an "advertisement" for your Civic Mission. Your display board should include your project's title and your name. You may then choose to post photos or any additional materials on your board. **SYNTHESIS**

2. Exhibit (3 points): Arrange your portfolio, t-shirt design, mobile of learning, and any additional materials you wish to include to create an appealing and informative overall exhibit. **SYNTHESIS**

COMPONENT 3:
Giving Your Classroom Presentation

Total Possible Classroom Presentation Points: 8 out of 100 total possible for project

1. What to Include in Your Presentation:

• Locality, Service Plan, and Event (1 point): Briefly explain your chosen locality, the basics of your service action plan, and your service event. **COMPREHENSION**

• Personal Perspectives (2 points): Share your personal challenge and inspirational message from Portfolio Section 3. **COMPREHENSION**

• Teach a Lesson (5 points): Create a brief fun lesson to teach your classmates one aspect of your academic goal that you learned during this process. **SYNTHESIS**

TEACHER COPY CHART

Step Number	Form Title	Number of Copies
1.1	Teacher Planning Guide	1 only
2.1-2.3	Parent Civic Mission Introduction Letter Student Civic Mission Introduction Letter Student Instruction Guide	1 completed, then 1 per student 1 completed only 1 only
3.1-3.4	Teacher Forms Checklist Student Commitment Contract	1 completed only 1 completed, then 1 per student
3.5	Student Civic Mission Introduction Letter* Student Instruction Guide* Civic Mission Resource Card Appendix Pages* (optional)	1 completed, then one per student 1 per student 1 per student
4.1-4.2	Student Checkpoint Organizer Teacher Checkpoint Record	1 per student 1 completed only
5.1-5.2	Student Expo Invitation	1 completed, then one per student
5.9-5.11	Student Certificate Student Name Sign (optional) Left Arrow Sign Right Arrow Sign	1 per student, then each completed 1 per student, then each completed Amount needed Amount needed
5.12-5.13	Teacher Assessment Student Self-Assessment	1 per student 1 per student

* Staple these items into a packet for each student

TEACHER PLANING GUIDE

Events scheduled with the class are in black.

Week	Event (Step Numbers)	Day and Date	Time
1	Planning and Preparing for the Quarter (1.1-1.2)		
	Prepare for Civic Mission Introduction (2.1-2.3)		
	Civic Mission Introduction (2.4-2.7)		
	Preparation for Civic Mission Implementation (3.1-3.6)		
	Civic Mission Implementation (3.7-3.17)		
3	Preparation for the Checkpoint Meetings (4.1-4.2)		
	Distribute Checkpoint Organizers (4.3-4.6)		
	Checkpoint Meetings (4.7-4.12)		
5	Preparation for the Checkpoint Meetings (4.1-4.2)		
	Distribute Checkpoint Organizers (4.3-4.6)		
	Checkpoint Meetings (4.7-4.12)		
7	Preparation for the Checkpoint Meetings (4.1-4.2)		
	Distribute Checkpoint Organizers (4.3-4.6)		
	Checkpoint Meetings (4.7-4.12)		
8	Preparation for the Civic Mission Expo (5.1-5.2)		
	Invite Families to the Civic Mission Expo (5.3-5.4)		
	Preparation for the Civic Mission Expo Ctd. (5.5-5.11)		
9	Preparation for Classroom Presentations and the Civic Mission Expo (5.12-5.15)		
	Classroom Presentations (6A.1-6A.13 or 6B.1-6B.12)		
	Classroom Expo and Student Self-Assessment (7A.1-7A.9 or 7B.1-7B.10)		
10	Final Preparation for the Civic Mission Expo (8.1-8.10)		
	Civic Mission Expo (9.1-9.4)		
	Conclusion and Teacher Assessment (10.1-10.8)		
	Student Review (10.9-10.10)		

CIVIC MISSION

parent civic mission introduction letter

Dear Parent(s),

Welcome to Civic Mission, the third in a series of four Envision projects that will challenge and inspire your child. Civic Mission offers your child the opportunity to interact and learn within the community while performing a service.

After creating a personal interests and talents profile, your child will choose an academic goal and partner with a community representative of a chosen locality. Your child will assess the locality's needs and form a service action plan, then participate in a self-designed service learning event. Along the way, your child will develop a reflection journal, a t-shirt design, a personal post-project reflection, a creative thank-you card, a mobile of learning, a personal challenge essay, and an inspirational message. Your child will then teach an academic lesson to the class. Some of the materials generated from these tasks will go into a project portfolio; others will become part of a colorful and informative visual exhibit.

A Student Instruction Guide will guide your child, step by step, through the entire project. The Instruction Guide, though comprehensive, is designed to foster creativity, inventiveness, and independent problem solving. The Instruction Guide will also point your child to helpful resource cards, which will provide additional explanation, ideas, tips, and examples. These cards will be available to you child whenever he or she is in our classroom working on the project.

Civic Mission is designed to be worked on independently during class time, free time, and at home. By scheduling several Checkpoint Meeting dates throughout the quarter, I will be able to monitor each student's progress. On these dates, I will meet with each student to discuss accomplishments and plan goals for the next checkpoint. I will also address any difficulties students might be having.

Civic Mission will conclude with a Project Expo. The expo will be your child's opportunity to share his or her finished project with family, friends, and other guests. You will receive a detailed invitation to the Project Expo later in the quarter.

Dates to Remember:

Checkpoint 1: _____

Checkpoint 2: _____

Checkpoint 3: _____

Classroom Presentation: _____

Civic Mission Expo: _____ , _____

Sincerely,

_____

_____

CIVIC MISSION

student civic mission introduction letter

Dear Student,

Welcome to Civic Mission! This is the third of four projects you will embark on as part of your Envision Program experience. Civic Mission challenges you to interact and learn within your community while performing a service. It will be a voyage of personal discovery and an opportunity for you to learn about your role in your community.

After creating a personal interests and talents profile, you will choose an academic goal and partner with a community representative of a locality that you are interested in. You will then assess the locality's needs, form your service action plan, and participate in a self-designed service learning event. Along the way, you will develop a personal reflection journal, design a t-shirt, write an in-depth post-project reflection and a creative thank-you card, and create a mobile of learning. You will also write a personal challenge essay, develop an inspirational message, and teach an academic lesson to your peers.

As with the other projects, some of the materials you create will go into a project portfolio, and others will become part of a colorful and informative project exhibit. You will formally share your finished project with the class by giving a brief presentation. The project will conclude, as the others have, with a fun project expo, at which you will share your project with invited family, friends, and guests.

You will work on Civic Mission throughout the school day, during your free time, and at home. Generally, you will be expected to work on your own. You will consult with me periodically at Checkpoint Meetings to discuss your progress and receive guidance. Between the checkpoints, feel free to discuss your project with other Envision students.

The attached Student Instruction Guide contains all the information you will need to complete the required Civic Mission Project successfully. The Instruction Guide will continue to challenge you to be resourceful, organized, and to think at a higher level.

Dates to Remember:

Checkpoint 1: _____

Checkpoint 2: _____

Checkpoint 3: _____

Classroom Presentation: _____

Civic Mission Expo: _____ , _____

After reading this introduction, you are now ready to begin thinking about your Civic Mission and planning this great adventure. Good luck and have fun!

Sincerely,

_____

_____

**Building Your Project Portfolio • Creating Your Project Exhibit
Presenting Your Project • Attending the Expo**

BE CREATIVE!

IMPORTANT!

Available resource cards are denoted by a Civic Mission icon . When you see one of these icons, you will know that there is a corresponding resource card available that gives additional helpful information and depicts visual examples for your reference. Also be sure to visit www.mindvinepress.com, other trustworthy Internet sites, and library reference materials for additional resources and examples.

COMPONENT 1

Building Your Project Portfolio Total Possible Portfolio Points: 86 out of 100 total possible for project

For this project, your mission is to partner with a community representative from a locality of your choice and plan a service event to help address a need of that locality. With good communication and thorough planning, your Civic Mission will be far from impossible. Complete the numbered requirements below, in order, as they build upon one another and will guide you smoothly through this planning process.

Note: "Component 1: Building Your Civic Mission Portfolio" is separated into three sections: "Portfolio Section 1: Pre Civic Mission Event", "Portfolio Section 2: Civic Mission Event", and "Portfolio Section 3: Post Civic Mission Event".

Portfolio Section 1: Pre Civic Mission Event

1. Personal Interests and Talents Profile (5 points): Using the computer, create a list of activities that you enjoy or at which you excel. Your list may include anything you do recreationally, academically, or socially. Use the copy, cut, and paste tools to rearrange your list so that the activities you enjoy most and at which you succeed most are at the top of your list. Your list should then progress in order downward to the activities you like less or at which you are not as successful.

2. Academic Goal (4 points): Record a specific academic goal that you would like to accomplish through your Civic Mission project. It can be something completely new to you or a skill you would like to refine, but it must be academically based and measurable. Explain why you chose this goal.

3. Community Locality Ranking (4 points): Research community localities that fit your top interests and talents, could help accomplish your academic goal, and accept volunteer assistance. Rank them in order of those you would most like to serve.

4. Partnership Commitment (5 points): Beginning with your top-ranked locality choice, contact the person in charge of working with volunteers. Explain that you would like to assist with the locality's needs, and ask if you can work together to create a service-learning project that will benefit you both. Continue this process until you have a firm commitment from someone who will work with you. Highlight this locality on your list from number three above.

5. Service Need and Solution (5 points): Discuss your chosen locality's genuine needs with its contact person. Brainstorm solutions to the locality's various needs and write them down. Together choose and highlight one need and solution that you can realistically help with, that fits your time frame and your interests or talents, and that helps you reach your academic goal. Be sure that your contact person knows you will be doing most of the planning and legwork for this project. Also be sure to discuss and obtain permission for this solution with your parent before officially committing to the idea.

6. Service Action Plan (7 points): Carefully plan all of the steps you will need to take to prepare for, carry out, and complete your Civic Mission event. Plan your event with enough time to complete the Post Civic Mission Event objectives in Portfolio Section 3 below. Before proceeding, review your plans with the contact person at your locality to be sure that your plans will work. Also double-check everything with your parent. You may then proceed with implementing your plan.

7. Computer-Generated Reflection Journal (7 points): Using the computer, begin writing a Civic Mission reflection journal. Two to three times each week, reflect on what is happening in this process. Include your predictions, feelings, evaluations, progress on your academic goal, learning, and whatever else you would like. You may choose to add illustrations, photos, and mementos as well.

8. Computer-Designed T-Shirt (5 points): Using the computer, design a t-shirt that relates to your Civic Mission project and that you and other volunteers might wear. Your design should include both an original artistic aspect as well as a written message. This t-shirt design will be kept separate from your portfolio.

Portfolio Section 2: Civic Mission Event

1. Final Preparations (5 points): Double-check on any final preparations you need to complete before your Civic Mission event takes place. Confirm the final plans with your contact person. Discuss any safety procedures that you need to be aware of with your contact person. Also ask if there are any situations that you might need to be sensitive to while you work. Write any important or helpful information on a sheet of paper and include it with your service action plan.

2. Event Participation (8 points): With parent permission and supervision, participate in your chosen Civic Mission event. Follow your plan and do the best you can to help your community while accomplishing your goals. Enjoy yourself, take photos if you can, and try to go out of your comfort zone by doing things you might not normally do.

Portfolio Section 3: Post Civic Mission Event

1. Post-Event Reflection (8 points): In your reflection journal, write an in-depth entry about your Civic Mission event. Be sure to answer the following questions:

- How did your event strengthen your community and contribute to the common good?
- What types of personal growth took place for you?
- What did you learn about yourself, others, and the locality?
- Were your goals accomplished? Please explain.
- What special or unexpected events took place?
- Did you enjoy planning and participating in this event? Why or why not?
- What should you have done differently?
- Would you participate in future service-learning events? Give your reasoning.

2. 🎭 Creative Thank-You Card (5 points): Create a thank-you card for your community contact and the locality you served. Design the card so it is reflective of the event. Take photos of the card to include in your portfolio then send it, or wait to send it until after your project assessments have been completed.

3. 🎭 Mobile of Learning (5 points): Design and create an artistic mobile showing various aspects of learning that took place for you with specific regards to your academic goal. Create a title and label each artistic element. This mobile will be kept separate from your portfolio.

4. Personal Challenge Essay (4 points): Record a personal challenge you faced during this process and how you met that challenge.

5. Inspirational Message (4 points): Write about a moment that you will remember from this experience. Explain how that experience was meaningful to you in a way that might inspire others to become involved in service learning.

Remaining Portfolio Materials

1. 🎭 Table of Contents (2 points): Write a table of contents that lists all the sections of your portfolio along with their corresponding page numbers.

2. 🎭 Cover Page (1 point): Create an eye-catching cover page for your portfolio that includes an original title for your project as well as your name and the Classroom Presentation date.

3. 🎭 Portfolio (2 points): Organize all of your materials in a three-ring binder. The table of contents should come first, followed by your work from Portfolio Sections 1, 2, and 3 above in the order presented. Your cover page should go on the front of the portfolio.

You have completed Component 1 of the Civic Mission Project. By completing your portfolio, you have created an important resource that will help you work on Components 2 and 3. Though several worthy challenges lie ahead, you are now prepared to meet each of them, knowing that you have laid the necessary groundwork that will increase your chances for success. Good luck as you move on to creating your project exhibit items.

STUDENT INSTRUCTION GUIDE

COMPONENT 2
Creating Your Civic Mission Exhibit
Total Possible Exhibit Points: 6 out of 100 total possible for project

Having planned and experienced a successful service learning event, it is now time to design and create an informative and appealing exhibit of your work. The items you complete will be viewed by your classmates on the day of your Classroom Presentation and also by everyone who attends the Civic Mission Expo at the end of the term. As always, put your best work into designing, creating, and integrating your exhibit items.

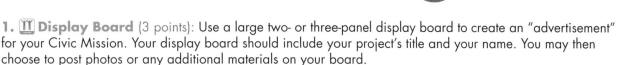

Note:
Keep in mind that each item is only one part of the overall exhibit. In other words, no single item has to say everything about your project. Decide upon a purpose for each item. Consider how best to arrange your exhibit for the greatest effect.

1. **Display Board** (3 points): Use a large two- or three-panel display board to create an "advertisement" for your Civic Mission. Your display board should include your project's title and your name. You may then choose to post photos or any additional materials on your board.

2. **Exhibit** (3 points): Arrange your portfolio, t-shirt design, mobile of learning, and any additional materials you wish to include to create an appealing and informative overall exhibit.

You have now completed Component 2 of the Civic Mission Project, giving you an important exhibit that creatively displays your mission and its results. Now that you have finished your portfolio and exhibit, you are ready to prepare for your Classroom Presentation (Component 3), during which you will share your project with your peers and teacher.

COMPONENT 3:

Giving Your Classroom Presentation

Total Possible Classroom Presentation Points: 8 out of 100 total possible for project

Now that you have positively affected your community and learned new things in the process, it is time to share your project with others. The Classroom Presentation is an opportunity to formally present your hard work with your classmates and teacher. Your portfolio and exhibit contain all the information you will need to prepare for the presentation, so relax and have fun.

1. 🛈 What to Include in Your Presentation:

- Locality, Service Plan, and Event (1 point): Briefly explain your chosen locality, the basics of your service action plan, and your service event.

- Personal Perspectives (2 points): Share your personal challenge and inspirational message from Portfolio Section 3.

- 🛈 Teach a Lesson (5 points): Create a brief fun lesson to teach your classmates one aspect of your academic goal that you learned during this process.

> **Note:** Your presentation should last between 3-4 minutes and should be rehearsed, but not memorized. If you forget to include information from one of the bullet points, your teacher will ask you the question so that you have a chance to answer it.

Bring to the Classroom Presentation:
All of your exhibit items and anything extra that you would like to enhance your exhibit.

You are now finished with Components 1, 2, and 3 – all of the assessed portions of your project. The final component, Attending the Civic Mission Expo, provides a festive closure to the Civic Mission Project.

COMPONENT 4:

Attending the Civic Mission Expo (The expo does not involve any points.)

Now that you have completed your project and presented it to your peers, it is time to share your work with family and friends at the Civic Mission Expo. The expo is an event that recognizes and celebrates the hard work you have done on your Civic Mission Project. At the expo, you will set up and stand by your exhibit as invited guests walk around informally and view the projects. Guests may ask you friendly questions about your project as they visit your exhibit, so have fun sharing the highlights of your mission with them.

Bring to the Expo: all of your exhibit items and anything extra that you think will enhance your exhibit.

CONGRATULATIONS ON YOUR COMPLETED CIVIC MISSION PROJECT!

TEACHER FORMS CHECKLIST

use this checklist to record forms submitted by the students

student name	student commitment contract	student checkpoint organizer 1	student checkpoint organizer 2	student checkpoint organizer 3	expo invitation response	
					number attending	special equip. needed
1.						
2.						
3.						
4.						
5.						
6.						
7.						
8.						
9.						
10.						
11.						
12.						
13.						
14.						
15.						
16.						
17.						
18.						
19.						
20.						
21.						
22.						
23.						
24.						
25.						

STUDENT COMMITMENT CONTRACT

expectations

project work time

I agree to:

- be responsible for following my Student Instruction Guide to do my work.
- keep track of all my project materials.
- work hard on Envision without disturbing others.
- save my unanswered questions until my teacher is free to talk.

checkpoint meetings

I will come prepared with:

- my Student Instruction Guide.
- my completed Student Checkpoint Organizer.
- all of my project materials.

important dates and times

Checkpoint 1: _____

Checkpoint 2: _____

Checkpoint 3: _____

Classroom Presentation: _____

Civic Mission Expo: _____

_____

signatures

I agree to:

- meet expectations on the dates listed above.
- complete each of the Civic Mission requirements to the best of my ability.
- bring my project work to school each day so that I can work on it during extra time.
- take my project work from school each night so that I can work on it at home.

I understand that the Envision Civic Mission Project is a special opportunity, and that if I do not meet the above expectations, I may be asked to return to normal classroom activities.

Student Signature: _____ Date: _____

Parent Signature: _____ Date: _____

Please return this contract by: _____

STUDENT CHECKPOINT ORGANIZER

Student Name: _____ Checkpoint Date: _____

Locality Choice: _____

Service Solution: _____

directions

1. Using your Student Instruction Guide, check off any requirements that you have completed up to this point.

2. Bring the following items to the Checkpoint Meeting:

• your Student Instruction Guide.

• your completed Student Checkpoint Organizer.

• all of your project materials.

questions

1. Which requirements have you completed up to this point?

_____

_____

2. Is there anything you need help with?

_____

_____

3. Is there anything else about your project that you would like to discuss?

_____

_____

4. List at least three goals you expect to accomplish by the next checkpoint.

_____

_____

TEACHER CHECKPOINT RECORD

student name	locality and solution choice	checkpoint 1 notes	checkpoint 2 notes	checkpoint 3 notes
1.				
2.				
3.				
4.				
5.				
6.				
7.				
8.				
9.				
10.				

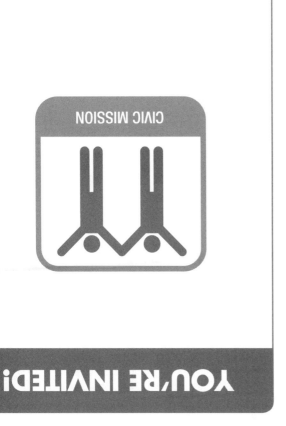

CIVIC MISSION

YOU'RE INVITED!

EXPO INVITATION RESPONSE

Please fill out and return by: _____

Student Name: _____

Student Attending? ☐ Yes ☐ No

Number of Student Guests Attending: _____

Will your child need any special school equipment for the expo (i.e., computer or TV)? Please List: _____

_____

Thank you.

We look forward to seeing you at this special event!

CIVIC MISSION

PLEASE JOIN US FOR OUR ENVISION CIVIC MISSION EXPO!

Why? _____

Who? _____

Where? _____

When? _____

Remember to bring your camera!

CIVIC MISSION

CERTIFICATE OF ACHIEVEMENT

CIVIC MISSION

AWARDED TO

DATE

SIGNATURE

envisiOn

CIVIC MISSION PROJECT

STUDENT

envision

civic mission expo

envision®

TEACHER ASSESSMENT

Component 1: Building Your Project Portfolio
Total Possible Portfolio Points: 86 out of 100 total possible for project

Requirements	Possible Points	Teacher Points	Average Points
Portfolio Section 1: Pre Civic Mission Event			
1. Personal Interests and Talents Profile: Using the computer, create a list of activities that you enjoy or at which you excel. Your list may include anything you do recreationally, academically, or socially. Use the copy, cut, and paste tools to rearrange your list so that the activities you enjoy most and at which you succeed most are at the top of your list. Your list should then progress in order downward to the activities you like less or at which you are not as successful.	5		
2. Academic Goal: Record a specific academic goal that you would like to accomplish through your Civic Mission project. It can be something completely new to you or a skill you would like to refine, but it must be academically based and measurable. Explain why you chose this goal.	4		
3. Community Locality Ranking: Research community localities that fit your top interests and talents, could help accomplish your academic goal, and accept volunteer assistance. Rank them in order of those you would most like to serve.	4		
4. Partnership Commitment: Beginning with your top-ranked locality choice, contact the person in charge of working with volunteers. Explain that you would like to assist with the locality's needs, and ask if you can work together to create a service-learning project that will benefit you both. Continue this process until you have a firm commitment from someone who will work with you. Highlight this locality on your list from number three above.	5		
5. Service Need and Solution: Discuss your chosen locality's genuine needs with its contact person. Brainstorm solutions to the locality's various needs and write them down. Together choose and highlight one need and solution that you can realistically help with, that fits your time frame and your interests or talents, and that helps you reach your academic goal. Be sure that your contact person knows you will be doing most of the planning and legwork for this project. Also be sure to discuss and obtain permission for this solution with your parent before officially committing to the idea.	5		
6. Service Action Plan: Carefully plan all of the steps you will need to take to prepare for, carry out, and complete your Civic Mission event. Plan your event with enough time to complete the Post Civic Mission Event objectives in Portfolio Section 3 below. Before proceeding, review your plans with the contact person at your locality to be sure that your plans will work. Also double-check everything with your parent. You may then proceed with implementing your plan.	7		
7. Computer-Generated Reflection Journal: Using the computer, begin writing a Civic Mission reflection journal. Two to three times each week, reflect on what is happening in this process. Include your predictions, feelings, evaluations, progress on your academic goal, learning, and whatever else you would like. You may choose to add illustrations, photos, and mementos as well.	7		

8. Computer-Designed T-Shirt: Using the computer, design a t-shirt that relates to your Civic Mission project and that you and other volunteers might wear. Your design should include both an original artistic aspect as well as a written message.	5		

Portfolio Section 2: Civic Mission Event

1. Final Preparations: Double-check on any final preparations you need to complete before your Civic Mission event takes place. Confirm the final plans with your contact person. Discuss any safety procedures that you need to be aware of with your contact person. Also ask if there are any situations that you might need to be sensitive to while you work. Write any important or helpful information on a sheet of paper and include it with your service action plan.	5		
2. Event Participation: With parent permission and supervision, participate in your chosen Civic Mission event. Follow your plan and do the best you can to help your community while accomplishing your goals. Enjoy yourself, take photos if you can, and try to go out of your comfort zone by doing things you might not normally do.	8		

Portfolio Section 3: Post Civic Mission Event

1. Post-Event Reflection: In your reflection journal, write an in-depth entry about your Civic Mission event. Be sure to answer the following questions: • How did your event strengthen your community and contribute to the common good? • What types of personal growth took place for you? • What did you learn about yourself, others, and the locality? • Were your goals accomplished? Please explain. • What special or unexpected events took place? • Did you enjoy planning and participating in this event? Why or why not? • What should you have done differently? • Would you participate in future service-learning events? Give your reasoning.	8		
2. Creative Thank-You Card: Create a thank-you card for your community contact and the locality you served. Design the card so it is reflective of the event. Take photos of the card to include in your portfolio then send it, or wait to send it until after your project assessments have been completed.	5		
3. Mobile of Learning: Design and create an artistic mobile showing various aspects of learning that took place for you with specific regards to your academic goal. Create a title and label each artistic element.	5		

4. Personal Challenge Essay: Record a personal challenge you faced during this process and how you met that challenge.	4		
5. Inspirational Message: Write about a moment that you will remember from this experience. Explain how that experience was meaningful to you in a way that might inspire others to become involved in service learning.	4		
Remaining Portfolio Materials			
1. Table of Contents: Write a table of contents that lists all the sections of your portfolio along with their corresponding page numbers.	2		
2. Cover Page: Create an eye-catching cover page for your portfolio that includes an original title for your project as well as your name and the Classroom Presentation date.	1		
3. Portfolio: Organize all of your materials in a three-ring binder. The table of contents should come first, followed by your work from Portfolio Sections 1, 2, and 3 above in the order presented. Your cover page should go on the front of the portfolio.	2		
TOTAL PORTFOLIO POINTS	**86**		

Component 2: Creating Your Civic Mission Exhibit
Total Possible Exhibit Points: 6 out of 100 total possible for project

1. Display Board: Use a large two- or three-panel display board to create an "advertisement" for your Civic Mission. Your display board should include your project's title and your name. You may then choose to post photos or any additional materials on your board.	3		
2. Exhibit: Arrange your portfolio, t-shirt design, mobile of learning, and any additional materials you wish to include to create an appealing and informative overall exhibit.	3		
TOTAL EXHIBIT POINTS	**6**		

Component 3: Giving Your Classroom Presentation
Total Possible Classroom Presentation Points: 8 out of 100 total possible for project

1. What to Include in Your Presentation:			
• Locality, Service Plan, and Event: Briefly explain your chosen locality, the basics of your service action plan, and your service event.	1		
• Personal Perspectives: Share your personal challenge and inspirational message from Portfolio Section 3.	2		
• Teach a Lesson: Create a brief fun lesson to teach your classmates one aspect of your academic goal that you learned during this process.	5		
TOTAL CLASSROOM PRESENTATION POINTS	**8**		
TOTAL PROJECT POINTS	**100**		

STUDENT SELF-ASSESSMENT

Component 1: Building Your Project Portfolio
Total Possible Portfolio Points: 86 out of 100 total possible for project

Requirements	Possible Points	Student Points
Portfolio Section 1: Pre Civic Mission Event		
1. Personal Interests and Talents Profile: Using the computer, create a list of activities that you enjoy or at which you excel. Your list may include anything you do recreationally, academically, or socially. Use the copy, cut, and paste tools to rearrange your list so that the activities you enjoy most and at which you succeed most are at the top of your list. Your list should then progress in order downward to the activities you like less or at which you are not as successful.	5	
2. Academic Goal: Record a specific academic goal that you would like to accomplish through your Civic Mission project. It can be something completely new to you or a skill you would like to refine, but it must be academically based and measurable. Explain why you chose this goal.	4	
3. Community Locality Ranking: Research community localities that fit your top interests and talents, could help accomplish your academic goal, and accept volunteer assistance. Rank them in order of those you would most like to serve.	4	
4. Partnership Commitment: Beginning with your top-ranked locality choice, contact the person in charge of working with volunteers. Explain that you would like to assist with the locality's needs, and ask if you can work together to create a service-learning project that will benefit you both. Continue this process until you have a firm commitment from someone who will work with you. Highlight this locality on your list from number three above.	5	
5. Service Need and Solution: Discuss your chosen locality's genuine needs with its contact person. Brainstorm solutions to the locality's various needs and write them down. Together choose and highlight one need and solution that you can realistically help with, that fits your time frame and your interests or talents, and that helps you reach your academic goal. Be sure that your contact person knows you will be doing most of the planning and legwork for this project. Also be sure to discuss and obtain permission for this solution with your parent before officially committing to the idea.	5	
6. Service Action Plan: Carefully plan all of the steps you will need to take to prepare for, carry out, and complete your Civic Mission event. Plan your event with enough time to complete the Post Civic Mission Event objectives in Portfolio Section 3 below. Before proceeding, review your plans with the contact person at your locality to be sure that your plans will work. Also double-check everything with your parent. You may then proceed with implementing your plan.	7	
7. Computer-Generated Reflection Journal: Using the computer, begin writing a Civic Mission reflection journal. Two to three times each week, reflect on what is happening in this process. Include your predictions, feelings, evaluations, progress on your academic goal, learning, and whatever else you would like. You may choose to add illustrations, photos, and mementos as well.	7	

8. Computer-Designed T-Shirt: Using the computer, design a t-shirt that relates to your Civic Mission project and that you and other volunteers might wear. Your design should include both an original artistic aspect as well as a written message.	5	
Portfolio Section 2: Civic Mission Event		
1. Final Preparations: Double-check on any final preparations you need to complete before your Civic Mission event takes place. Confirm the final plans with your contact person. Discuss any safety procedures that you need to be aware of with your contact person. Also ask if there are any situations that you might need to be sensitive to while you work. Write any important or helpful information on a sheet of paper and include it with your service action plan.	5	
2. Event Participation: With parent permission and supervision, participate in your chosen Civic Mission event. Follow your plan and do the best you can to help your community while accomplishing your goals. Enjoy yourself, take photos if you can, and try to go out of your comfort zone by doing things you might not normally do.	8	
Portfolio Section 3: Post Civic Mission Event		
1. Post-Event Reflection: In your reflection journal, write an in-depth entry about your Civic Mission event. Be sure to answer the following questions: • How did your event strengthen your community and contribute to the common good? • What types of personal growth took place for you? • What did you learn about yourself, others, and the locality? • Were your goals accomplished? Please explain. • What special or unexpected events took place? • Did you enjoy planning and participating in this event? Why or why not? • What should you have done differently? • Would you participate in future service-learning events? Give your reasoning.	8	
2. Creative Thank-You Card: Create a thank-you card for your community contact and the locality you served. Design the card so it is reflective of the event. Take photos of the card to include in your portfolio then send it, or wait to send it until after your project assessments have been completed.	5	
3. Mobile of Learning: Design and create an artistic mobile showing various aspects of learning that took place for you with specific regards to your academic goal. Create a title and label each artistic element.	5	

4. Personal Challenge Essay: Record a personal challenge you faced during this process and how you met that challenge.	4	
5. Inspirational Message: Write about a moment that you will remember from this experience. Explain how that experience was meaningful to you in a way that might inspire others to become involved in service learning.	4	
Remaining Portfolio Materials		
1. Table of Contents: Write a table of contents that lists all the sections of your portfolio along with their corresponding page numbers.	2	
2. Cover Page: Create an eye-catching cover page for your portfolio that includes an original title for your project as well as your name and the Classroom Presentation date.	1	
3. Portfolio: Organize all of your materials in a three-ring binder. The table of contents should come first, followed by your work from Portfolio Sections 1, 2, and 3 above in the order presented. Your cover page should go on the front of the portfolio.	2	
TOTAL PORTFOLIO POINTS	**86**	

Component 2: Creating Your Civic Mission Exhibit
Total Possible Exhibit Points: 6 out of 100 total possible for project

1. Display Board: Use a large two- or three-panel display board to create an "advertisement" for your Civic Mission. Your display board should include your project's title and your name. You may then choose to post photos or any additional materials on your board.	3	
2. Exhibit: Arrange your portfolio, t-shirt design, mobile of learning, and any additional materials you wish to include to create an appealing and informative overall exhibit.	3	
TOTAL EXHIBIT POINTS	**6**	

Component 3: Giving Your Classroom Presentation
Total Possible Classroom Presentation Points: 8 out of 100 total possible for project

1. What to Include in Your Presentation:		
• Locality, Service Plan, and Event: Briefly explain your chosen locality, the basics of your service action plan, and your service event.	1	
• Personal Perspectives: Share your personal challenge and inspirational message from Portfolio Section 3.	2	
• Teach a Lesson: Create a brief fun lesson to teach your classmates one aspect of your academic goal that you learned during this process.	5	
TOTAL CLASSROOM PRESENTATION POINTS	**8**	
TOTAL PROJECT POINTS	**100**	

EXAMPLE
CIVIC MISSION
STUDENT RESOURCE CARDS

PERSONAL INTERESTS AND TALENTS PROFILE

When making a decision, it can be helpful to create a list that you can evaluate and rank. This process often helps to put your priorities in perspective and narrow your choices.

When making your list on the computer, start by brainstorming your activity choices in any order, recording each activity on a new line. Once you have completed each list, use the copy, paste, and cut tools to rearrange your list. To begin, highlight and copy an activity and paste it in a new position within your list. Once the activity is where you want it, you can highlight and cut the originally listed activity so that it is not listed twice. Continue this process until the activities you enjoy most and at which you succeed most are at the top of your list. Your list should then progress in order down to the activities you like less or at which you are not as successful.

Original Brainstorm	Copy to Clipboard	Paste into Final List
Biking	Collecting rocks	Collecting rocks
Cooking	Biking	Walking
Walking	Cooking	Cooking
Talking	Walking	Sewing
Serving	Talking	Talking
Cleaning	Serving	Skateboarding
Skateboarding	Cleaning	Reading
Sewing	Skateboarding	Biking
Singing	Sewing	Singing
Reading	Singing	Cleaning
Collecting rocks	Reading	Serving

EXAMPLE

ACADEMIC GOAL

Having a specific academic goal to accomplish during your Civic Mission experience will add to the overall growth you achieve through this process. Your goal can be related to any academic area, but it should be challenging and attainable.

When you write your academic goal, think about skills that you would like to learn or improve, and choose one that fits the above criteria. Write your goal clearly and in a way that is measurable. Remember to explain why you chose your specific goal.

Goals That Are Clear and Measurable
Compute five cash register receipts correctly.
Identify six birds that are new to me.
Demonstrate the ballot-counting process in my city.
Read, pronounce, and define ten new Spanish words.
Write three letters using correct formatting.
Create a tri-fold brochure using the computer.

Goals That Are Unclear and Not Measurable
Learn how to use a cash register.
Study some new birds.
See how voting ballots are counted.
Practice my Spanish.
Improve at writing letters.
Find out how create a brochure using the computer.

EXAMPLE

WAYNE'S ACADEMIC GOAL

Identify six birds that are new to me.
I chose this goal because I...

SERVICE ACTION PLAN

Organizing an action plan is an important part of creating, carrying out, and completing a successful event. An action plan will help you organize the details of your event so that you are prepared and things run smoothly.

Start by writing your main goal or goals for your event. Next, record every step that must be taken to accomplish each goal. To determine tasks that must be accomplished you should consider: dates, time frame, location and space, weather factors, numbers of participants and helpers needed, supplies, costs, funding ideas, safety, pre-preparation, set-up, clean-up, and transportation. Always keep the need, solution, and your goals in mind as you plan. Write your plan in the format that works best for you. It may be a table, web, calendar, or a combination of these.

Suzie's Main Goal #1:

Date: January 8, 2XXX
Time: 5pm – 9pm
Location: cafeteria of Shady Acres
Rain location: N/A

Number of Participants: 25
Number of Helpers: 7

EXAMPLE

Supplies we'll need: cups, bowls, spoons...
Total cost of supplies: $72.81
Funding will come from: Shady Acres

Complete before the event: purchase supplies, make...
Set-up before the event: hang streamers...
Clean-up after the event: take down streamers...

I will get there by: My dad will drive me there, stay with me to help, and drive me home.

COMPUTER-GENERATED T-SHIRT DESIGN

Often, people create t-shirts to celebrate or create awareness for an event. Once the event has been completed, it serves as a pleasant reminder and conversation piece when it is worn. T-shirts can be informative, funny, serious, or artistic. The back of the shirt can be decorated in addition to the front of the shirt. The computer can be used to make the design and then it can be printed on special iron-on paper. After printing the design it can be ironed onto a t-shirt with the help of a parent.

When designing your t-shirt's art and message, be sure that its tone corresponds with the tone of your event. Usually, people include the date and title of the event. Sometimes they also include participant names, sponsor names, or activities for the event.

EXAMPLE

THE SUNSHINE WALK

DAISY PARK

CREATIVE THANK-YOU CARD

It is customary to send a thank-you card to people who do something for you or allow you to do something. In this case, sending an informal thank-you card to your contact person and the locality or organization you helped would be an appropriate gesture.

The format of an informal thank-you card can vary widely depending on the situation. Your thank you card may be any size, use any colors, and may be folded, flat, or three-dimensional. You should include the date, a salutation, a body, and a closing. Show appreciation for specific actions and make it personal.

Thank You Woodland Hills!

Dear Ms. Blake and Staff,

Thank you very much for…

I truly enjoyed…

Sincerely,

Melanie Bondy

January 29, 2XXX

EXAMPLE

MOBILE OF LEARNING

A mobile is a three-dimensional sculpture that uses rods and other materials to hang artistic representations in balance with each other at varying heights. Mobiles are usually eye-catching, and when they are hung the artistic representations gently spin to show all sides.

Think about what you learned during your service learning experience with regards to your academic goal. As you design the artistic elements that capture your academic learning, give each one a label. Please title your mobile.

Eian's Spanish Growth

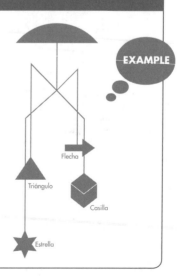

EXAMPLE

Flecha

Triángulo

Casilla

Estrella

TABLE OF CONTENTS

Your table of contents should be the first page in your portfolio, although you write it after you finish all of the pages inside. Writing it after finishing the contents allows you to be accurate with your page numbers and titles in case you make any last-minute changes. Your table of contents should list each section and the page it begins on. It should be neat and well organized, but feel free to be creative with your own layout.

EXAMPLE

TABLE OF CONTENTS

Page Number	Section Title
1	Personal Interests and Talents Profile
2	Academic Goal
3	Community Locality Ranking
4	Service Need and Solution
5-9	Service Action Plan
10-18	Computer-Generated Reflection Journal

COVER PAGE

The cover page of your portfolio acts like the cover of a book. It should be eye-catching and should make someone want to open your portfolio to read about your project. It should include an original title for your project as well as your name and the Classroom Presentation date. Feel free to be creative and include artwork, design, and other creative touches.

FRONT COVER   SPINE   BACK COVER

EXAMPLE

PAINTING FOR A CAUSE!

4·8·XX
BY JOE

PAINTING FOR A CAUSE!

WE PAINTED.
WE GOT MESSY.
WE HELPED CREATE A
DREAM!

PORTFOLIO

Your portfolio is what you will use to organize most of your paper items. A standard one- to one-and-a-half-inch binder with a clear plastic overlay works well. Arrange the contents of the portfolio in the order that they are mentioned in your Student Instruction Guide. The cover should include your name, Classroom Presentation date, and an original project title. You may wish to add tab dividers for each section listed in your table of contents, clear page protectors for each piece of paper, and creative personal touches.

EXAMPLE

DISPLAY BOARD

The purpose of your display board is to draw attention to your project and to highlight some of its interesting information. It should be creative and colorful while remaining neat and well organized. Remember to make sure that it contains the necessary items listed on your Student Instruction Guide including your project's title and your name. The example below is to be used only as a guide; feel free to demonstrate your creativity. Tip: two- or three-panel display boards can be purchased at most craft stores. If you would rather make one, you can ask an adult to help construct one from a large cardboard box.

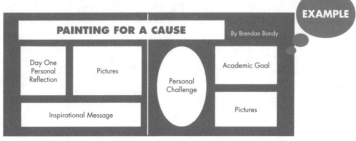

EXHIBIT

The purpose of your exhibit is to draw people's attention to your project. It should be neat, colorful, and creative. Your exhibit should include the items required in Component 2 of your Student Instruction Guide and any additional materials you wish to bring. The example below is to be used only as a guide; feel free to rearrange.

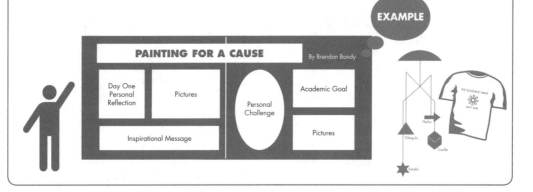

WHAT TO INCLUDE IN YOUR PRESENTATION

Your presentation will be a talk on what you learned, experienced, and produced for your project. It will also include your teaching a brief lesson to your peers. You should practice until you are comfortable with what you will say, but do not memorize a speech. Your presentation should be three to four minutes long and address the bulleted information listed in Component 3 of your Student Instruction Guide.

REMEMBER TO:

- Take a deep breath, relax, and enjoy sharing.
- Greet your audience and introduce yourself.
- Speak clearly, loudly enough so everyone can hear you, and at a natural pace.
- Stand still and calm; don't fidget.
- Point to and show various visuals as you speak about them.
- Make eye contact with your audience, looking around the room naturally.
- Thank your audience when you are finished.

TEACH A LESSON

When teaching a lesson, it is a good idea to begin with something that will get your audience's attention. It can be a visual, a question, or an odd statement. Once you have their attention, you should try to relate your upcoming lesson to something they are familiar with. By doing this, you allow your audience to become comfortable and open to what you are about to teach them.

Choosing an objective, or what you want your audience to learn, is the first step in creating the actual lesson. After you have chosen an objective, come up with a fun creative, preferably active, way of teaching that objective to your audience. An objective can be taught by using a song, play, story, dance, experiment, demonstration, or game. Rehearse your entire lesson several times so that your presentation is smooth, understandable, and fun.

CLASS IN SESSION

APPENDIX 4:
FITNESS PURSUIT FORMS AND
RESOURCE CARDS

Levels From Lowest to Highest:
KNOWLEDGE • COMPREHENSION • APPLICATION • ANALYSIS • EVALUATION • SYNTHESIS

Below you will find each Fitness Pursuit requirement, along with its corresponding level of Bloom's Taxonomy.

> **IMPORTANT!**
> The levels listed above are cumulative. For example, the highest level of thinking, Synthesis, incorporates all other levels of thinking: Knowledge, Comprehension, Application, Analysis, and Evaluation.

COMPONENT 1
Building Your Fitness Pursuit Portfolio
Total Possible Portfolio Points: 81 out of 100 total possible for project

Portfolio Section 1: Sleep Health

1. Sleep Log (6 points): For at least 14 days, keep a log of your sleep habits. Record your sleep amounts including any naps. Each evening before bed, reflect on and record how you felt throughout that day and give it a rating in your log. Include a key for your rating scale. **EVALUATION**

2. Computer-Generated Double Line Graph (5 points): Using the computer, create a double line graph that shows every day you recorded in your sleep log, the hours of sleep you received for each, and your rating for each day. Include a graph title, a key, and your sleep log rating scale. **SYNTHESIS**

3. Graph Analysis and Goal (5 points): Analyze your graph and below it write about any consistent patterns you notice. **ANALYSIS** Using those observations, draw various conclusions about the ways different sleep patterns affect how you feel. Based on your conclusions, determine what you think is your personal optimal amount of daily sleep and state that as a goal. Discuss this with your parent. **SYNTHESIS**

4. Sleep Goal Room Art (5 points): Create a piece of art that you can display in your bedroom. Your artwork should remind you of sleeping and should display your parent-approved sleep goal amount. **SYNTHESIS**

Portfolio Section 2: Healthy Eating

1. Healthy Eating Investigation (5 points): Investigate healthy eating recommendations for each main food group based on your gender, age, and size. Record recommended daily amounts for each group, and note specific food examples within each. **COMPREHENSION** Be sure that your sources are reliable and substantiated. Some reliable sources are health care providers and governmental health agencies. Record your findings along with your information sources and analyze them for commonalities. Highlight the commonalities within each group. **ANALYSIS**

2. Personal Food Pyramid (5 points): Design and illustrate a detailed, daily food pyramid based on the commonalities you found in your healthy eating investigation. Be creative and make the pyramid attractive in contents and appearance. Share it with your parent. **SYNTHESIS**

3. Healthy Eating Regimen (6 points): Using your personal food pyramid, plan one week's worth of optimal meals and snacks for yourself. You may organize it any way you wish. Take into account regular activities such as eating at school and participating in after-school activities. Review this plan with your parent who can help analyze it with respect to your personal health and lifestyle. **SYNTHESIS**

Portfolio Section 3: Physical Health

1. Personal Exercise Guidelines (4 points): Examine exercise recommendations for your gender, age, and size including types of exercise and the duration of activity. Be sure that your sources are reliable and substantiated. Some source ideas are health care providers and governmental health agencies. Based on your findings, decide on general weekly personal guidelines for types of exercise and the durations of each activity. Explain your reasoning. Discuss this with your parent. **SYNTHESIS**

2. Health Benefits Sentence Scramble (5 points): Investigate and record various health benefits of physical exercise. **COMPREHENSION** Read your information and choose what you think are the top ten benefits. **EVALUATION** Create a sentence scramble of ten sentences, each describing a benefit you chose. Include an answer key, write a title, and record directions for someone who might try your sentence scramble. **SYNTHESIS**

3. Exercise Duration Clocks (5 points): Draw two non-digital clocks on a piece of paper. Label one "Weekdays" and label one "Weekends." On each clock, first draw the hands of the clock to show the time of day that you might begin an exercise activity. Next on each clock, shade the clock from your start time to the time you might stop the activity. Label the total duration times below each clock, making sure they correspond with your personal exercise guidelines. Lastly, write the name of a few activities you might choose to do during each exercise period. Share these with your parent. **APPLICATION**

4. Safety Test (5 points): Create a test and answer key that assesses understanding of various age-appropriate safety issues. Some examples are bicycle and road safety, stranger safety, Internet safety, and safety in public places. Give the test to at least three peers and your parent. Correct the papers and review the results with each person. **SYNTHESIS**

Portfolio Section 4: Healthy Brain

1. Academic Activity List (6 points): Make a list of academic activities that you would like to become better at or try for the first time. Your hobbies should be activities that help improve your academic knowledge base in various subject areas. Some examples are: rock collecting and identification, mystery reading, learning about various shipwrecks, playing chess, writing a novel, or woodworking. **EVALUATION** Label each activity according to the ideal season in which you can participate in it. **EVALUATION** Reorganize your list so that you have two to three activities, listed in order of preference, in each seasonal subcategory. **SYNTHESIS**

2. Academic Activity List Personalization (4 points): For each academic activity you listed, think of something specific and personally interesting that you can keep track of, and write it with its corresponding activity. For example, beside "Rock Collecting" you might write, "My List of Favorite Rocks" or for solving logic puzzles you might write, "Current Best Time in Seconds." **APPLICATION**

3. Weekly Homework Schedule (5 points): Create a schedule of a typical week and your main activities such as school, meals, sports, and other activities. Looking at each day's activities, set aside a daily block of time when you will do your homework. Take into consideration the typical amount of time your teachers and parents advise that you should be spending on homework on each weekday and also on weekends. **SYNTHESIS**

4. Stress and Calm Match-Up Illustration (5 points): To round out your total health plan, you will also consider stress in your life and how you might handle it. On the left side of a sheet of paper progressing downward, draw and label pictures of things that are stressful to you. **ANALYSIS** On the right side of the paper, but not in the same order, draw and label pictures of something you can do to calm yourself in each situation. Draw a line from each stressful event to its appropriate calming solution to show your answers. **SYNTHESIS**

Remaining Portfolio Materials

1. Table of Contents (2 points): Write a table of contents that lists all the sections of your portfolio along with their corresponding page numbers. **COMPREHENSION**

2. Cover Page (1 point): Create an eye-catching cover page for your portfolio that includes an original title for your project as well as your name and the Classroom Presentation date. **SYNTHESIS**

3. Portfolio (2 points): Organize all of your materials in a three-ring binder. The table of contents should come first, followed by your work from Portfolio Sections 1, 2, 3, and 4 above in the order presented. Your cover page should go on the front of the portfolio. **SYNTHESIS**

COMPONENT 2

Creating Your Fitness Pursuit Exhibit

Total Possible Exhibit Points: 14 out of 100 total possible for project

1. One-Month Master Calendar (8 points): Create a large one-month calendar showing each day of the month. Using a pencil, record all of your new goals for sleep health, healthy eating, physical health, and a healthy brain. Review this calendar with your parent. **SYNTHESIS**

2. Display Board (3 points): Use a large two- or three-panel display board to create an "advertisement" for your Fitness Pursuit. It must include your one-month calendar, your project's title, and your name. You may then choose to add any of the required items or any additional materials that you wish. **SYNTHESIS**

3. Exhibit (3 points): Arrange your portfolio, sleep goal room art, and any additional materials you wish to include in an appealing and informative way. **SYNTHESIS**

COMPONENT 3:

Giving Your Classroom Presentation

Total Possible Classroom Presentation Points: 5 out of 100 total possible for project

1. What to Include in Your Presentation:

- Sleep Goal Room Art (1 point): Share the art piece you designed for your room and explain how you decided upon your sleep goal. **COMPREHENSION**

- Personal Food Pyramid (1 point): Show your food pyramid. Tell the class which portions will be the most difficult for you to attain each day and explain how you plan to meet those goals. **SYNTHESIS**

- Safety Test (1 point): Ask the class an important question from your safety test and see if anyone can answer it correctly. **COMPREHENSION**

- Academic Activities List and Personalization (2 points): Explain one of your academic activities to the class. Share how you will personalize it for yourself. **COMPREHENSION**

TEACHER COPY CHART

Step Number	Form Title	Number of Copies
1.1	Teacher Planning Guide	1 only
2.1-2.3	Parent Fitness Pursuit Introduction Letter Student Fitness Pursuit Introduction Letter Student Instruction Guide	1 completed, then 1 per student 1 completed only 1 only
3.1-3.4	Teacher Forms Checklist Student Commitment Contract	1 completed only 1 completed, then 1 per student
3.5	Student Fitness Pursuit Introduction Letter* Student Instruction Guide* Fitness Pursuit Resource Card Appendix Pages* (optional)	1 completed, then one per student 1 per student 1 per student
4.1-4.2	Student Checkpoint Organizer Teacher Checkpoint Record	1 per student 1 completed only
5.1-5.2	Student Expo Invitation	1 completed, then one per student
5.9-5.11	Student Certificate Student Name Sign (optional) Left Arrow Sign Right Arrow Sign	1 per student, then each completed 1 per student, then each completed Amount needed Amount needed
5.12-5.13	Teacher Assessment Student Self-Assessment	1 per student 1 per student

* Staple these items into a packet for each student

TEACHER PLANING GUIDE

Events scheduled with the class are in black.

Week	Event (Step Numbers)	Day and Date	Time
1	Planning and Preparing for the Quarter (1.1-1.2)		
	Prepare for Fitness Pursuit Introduction (2.1-2.3)		
	Fitness Pursuit Introduction Day (2.4-2.7)		
	Preparation for Fitness Pursuit Implementation (3.1-3.6)		
	Fitness Pursuit Implementation Day (3.7-3.17)		
3	Preparation for the Checkpoint Meetings (4.1-4.2)		
	Distribute Checkpoint Organizers (4.3-4.6)		
	Checkpoint Meeting Day (4.7-4.12)		
5	Preparation for the Checkpoint Meetings (4.1-4.2)		
	Distribute Checkpoint Organizers (4.3-4.6)		
	Checkpoint Meeting Day (4.7-4.12)		
7	Preparation for the Checkpoint Meetings (4.1-4.2)		
	Distribute Checkpoint Organizers (4.3-4.6)		
	Checkpoint Meeting Day (4.7-4.12)		
8	Preparation for the Fitness Pursuit Expo (5.1-5.2)		
	Invite Families to the Fitness Pursuit Expo (5.3-5.4)		
	Preparation for the Fitness Pursuit Expo Ctd. (5.5-5.11)		
9	Preparation for Classroom Presentations and the Fitness Pursuit Expo (5.12-5.15)		
	Classroom Presentations Day (6A.1-6A.13 or 6B.1-6B.12)		
	Classroom Expo and Student Self-Assessment Day (7A.1-7A.9 or 7B.1-7B.10)		
10	Final Preparation for the Fitness Pursuit Expo (8.1-8.10)		
	Fitness Pursuit Expo Day (9.1-9.4)		
	Conclusion and Teacher Assessment (10.1-10.8)		
	Student Review (10.9-10.10)		

FITNESS PURSUIT

parent fitness pursuit introduction letter

Dear Parent(s),

Welcome to Fitness Pursuit, the fourth of four Envision projects that will challenge and inspire your child. Fitness Pursuit will guide your child to develop an in-depth plan of healthy habits by which to live. Your child will have the opportunity to research four major areas of personal health and create numerous, unique visual elements as guides to healthy living.

For this project, your child will create a sleep log that will lead to generating a graph, a sleep goal, and a piece of room art. Your child will also investigate healthy eating habits, design a personal food pyramid, and plan a healthy eating regimen. Physical health will also be addressed by your child. He or she will look into and decide on personal exercise guidelines as well as design a safety test after researching various age-appropriate safety issues. Your child's portfolio will be rounded out with a Healthy Brain section that addresses personal academic activity pursuits, a weekly homework schedule, and an analysis of personally stressful situations and how to deal with them. For the exhibit, your child will create a one-month master calendar and arrange a display board highlighting some of his or her creations. Lastly, your child will give a brief formal presentation to the class.

A Student Instruction Guide will be provided to guide your child, step by step, through this process. The instruction guide is a comprehensive list of project requirements and is designed to engage higher-level thinking. The guide also references helpful resource cards, that provide additional explanation, ideas, tips, and directions. There will be a set of these cards in our classroom to which your child may refer.

Fitness Pursuit is designed to be worked on independently during class time, free time, and at home. By scheduling several Checkpoint Meeting dates throughout the quarter, I will be able to monitor each student's progress. On these dates, I will meet with each student to discuss accomplishments and plan goals for the next checkpoint. I will also address any difficulties students might be having.

Fitness Pursuit will conclude with a Project Expo. The expo will be your child's opportunity to share his or her finished project with family, friends, and other guests. You will receive a detailed invitation to the Project Expo later in the quarter.

Dates to Remember:

Checkpoint 1: _____

Checkpoint 2: _____

Checkpoint 3: _____

Classroom Presentation: _____

Fitness Pursuit Expo: _____ , _____

Sincerely,

_____

_____

student fitness pursuit introduction letter

Dear Student,

Welcome to Fitness Pursuit! This is the fourth of four projects you will embark on as part of the Envision Program experience. Fitness Pursuit is about cultivating an in-depth plan of healthy habits by which to live. It will be a voyage of personal discovery and an opportunity to set specific goals and design detailed plans that will directly affect your health both now and in the future.

The project begins with an analysis of your personal sleep habits. You will use this information to generate a graph, a sleep goal, and a piece of room art. You will also have the opportunity to develop a personal food pyramid, plan a healthy eating regimen, decide on personal exercise guidelines, design a safety test, construct a personal academic activities list, create a match-up illustration, and produce a calendar.

This project contains four components. The first is to organize your research and project materials in a project portfolio. The second will be to create an exhibit of your topic and findings. The third will be to share your completed portfolio and exhibit with your classmates. To do this, you will give a brief formal presentation. During your presentation, you will explain key aspects of your fitness findings and share various project components you created. The fourth is the Project Expo, an event that celebrates your hard work and achievements. This final component allows you the opportunity to invite family and friends to share in your success.

You will work on Fitness Pursuit throughout the school day, during your free time, and at home. Generally, you will be expected to work on your own. You will consult with me periodically at Checkpoint Meetings to discuss your progress and receive guidance. Between the checkpoints, feel free to discuss your project with other Envision students.

The attached Student Instruction Guide contains all the information you will need to complete the required Fitness Pursuit Project successfully. The instruction guide will challenge you to be resourceful, organized, and to think at a higher level.

Dates to Remember:

Checkpoint 1: _____

Checkpoint 2: _____

Checkpoint 3: _____

Classroom Presentation: _____

Fitness Pursuit Expo: _____ , _____

After reading this introduction, you are now ready to begin thinking about your personal overall fitness. Good luck!

Sincerely,

_____

_____

Building Your Project Portfolio • Creating Your Project Exhibit
Presenting Your Project • Attending the Expo

BE CREATIVE!

IMPORTANT!

Resource cards are denoted by a Fitness Pursuit icon . When you see one of these icons, you will know that there is a corresponding resource card available that gives additional helpful information and examples. Also, be sure to visit www.mindvinepress.com, other trustworthy Internet sites, various newspapers, and library reference materials for helpful resources and examples.

COMPONENT 1

Building Your Fitness Pursuit Portfolio

Total Possible Portfolio Points: 81 out of 100 total possible for project

You are about to cultivate an in-depth awareness of personal healthy habits to live by. This will be an opportunity to engage your curiosity, research new information, and make meaningful choices that will directly affect your personal health now and in the future. Complete the numbered requirements below in order, as they build upon one another to guide you smoothly through the project.

Note:
"Component 1: Building Your Project Portfolio" is separated into four sections: "Portfolio Section 1: Sleep Health," "Portfolio Section 2: Healthy Eating," "Portfolio Section 3: Physical Health," and "Portfolio Section 4: Healthy Brain".

Portfolio Section 1: Sleep Health

1. Sleep Log (6 points): For at least 14 days, keep a log of your sleep habits. Record your sleep amounts including any naps. Each evening before bed, reflect on and record how you felt throughout that day and give it a rating in your log. Include a key for your rating scale.

2. Computer-Generated Double Line Graph (5 points): Using the computer, create a double line graph that shows every day you recorded in your sleep log, the hours of sleep you received for each, and your rating for each day. Include a graph title, a key, and your sleep log rating scale.

3. Graph Analysis and Goal (5 points): Analyze your graph and below it write about any consistent patterns you notice. Using those observations, draw various conclusions about the ways different sleep patterns affect how you feel. Based on your conclusions, determine what you think is your personal optimal amount of daily sleep and state that as a goal. Discuss this with your parent.

4. Sleep Goal Room Art (5 points): Create a piece of art that you can display in your bedroom. Your artwork should remind you of sleeping and should display your parent-approved sleep goal amount. This art will be kept separate from your portfolio.

Portfolio Section 2: Healthy Eating

1. Healthy Eating Investigation (5 points): Investigate healthy eating recommendations for each main food group based on your gender, age, and size. Record recommended daily amounts for each group, and note specific food examples within each. Be sure that your sources are reliable and substantiated. Some reliable sources are health care providers and governmental health agencies. Record your findings along with your information sources and analyze them for commonalities. Highlight the commonalities within each group.

2. Personal Food Pyramid (5 points): Design and illustrate a detailed, daily food pyramid based on the commonalities you found in your healthy eating investigation. Be creative and make the pyramid attractive in contents and appearance. Share it with your parent.

3. Healthy Eating Regimen (6 points): Using your personal food pyramid, plan one week's worth of optimal meals and snacks for yourself. You may organize it any way you wish. Take into account regular activities such as eating at school and participating in after-school activities. Review this plan with your parent who can help analyze it with respect to your personal health and lifestyle.

Portfolio Section 3: Physical Health

1. Personal Exercise Guidelines (4 points): Examine exercise recommendations for your gender, age, and size including types of exercise and the duration of activity. Be sure that your sources are reliable and substantiated. Some source ideas are health care providers and governmental health agencies. Based on your findings, decide on general weekly personal guidelines for types of exercise and the durations of each activity. Explain your reasoning. Discuss this with your parent.

2. Health Benefits Sentence Scramble (5 points): Investigate and record various health benefits of physical exercise. Read your information and choose what you think are the top ten benefits. Create a sentence scramble of ten sentences, each describing a benefit you chose. Include an answer key, write a title, and record directions for someone who might try your sentence scramble.

3. 🚲 **Exercise Duration Clocks** (5 points): Draw two non-digital clocks on a piece of paper. Label one "Weekdays" and label one "Weekends." On each clock, first draw the hands of the clock to show the time of day that you might begin an exercise activity. Next on each clock, shade the clock from your start time to the time you might stop the activity. Label the total duration times below each clock, making sure they correspond with your personal exercise guidelines. Lastly, write the name of a few activities you might choose to do during each exercise period. Share these with your parent.

4. Safety Test (5 points): Create a test and answer key that assesses understanding of various age-appropriate safety issues. Some examples are bicycle and road safety, stranger safety, Internet safety, and safety in public places. Give the test to at least three peers and your parent. Correct the papers and review the results with each person.

Portfolio Section 4: Healthy Brain

1. Academic Activity List (6 points): Make a list of academic activities that you would like to become better at or try for the first time. Your hobbies should be activities that help improve your academic knowledge base in various subject areas. Some examples are: rock collecting and identification, mystery reading, learning about various shipwrecks, playing chess, writing a novel, or woodworking. Label each activity according to the ideal season in which you can participate in it. Reorganize your list so that you have two to three activities, listed in order of preference, in each seasonal subcategory.

2. Academic Activity List Personalization (4 points): For each academic activity you listed, think of something specific and personally interesting that you can keep track of, and write it with its corresponding activity. For example, beside "Rock Collecting" you might write, "My List of Favorite Rocks" or for solving logic puzzles you might write, "Current Best Time in Seconds."

3. Weekly Homework Schedule (5 points): Create a schedule of a typical week and your main activities such as school, meals, sports, and other activities. Looking at each day's activities, set aside a daily block of time when you will do your homework. Take into consideration the typical amount of time your teachers and parents advise that you should be spending on homework each weekday and also on weekends.

4. 🚲 **Stress and Calm Match-Up Illustration** (5 points): To round out your total health plan, you will also consider stress in your life and how you might handle it. On the left side of a sheet of paper progressing downward, draw and label pictures of things that are stressful to you. On the right side of the paper, but not in the same order, draw and label pictures of something you can do to calm yourself in each situation. Draw a line from each stressful event to its appropriate calming solution to show your answers.

Remaining Portfolio Materials

1. 🚲 **Table of Contents** (2 points): Write a table of contents that lists all the sections of your portfolio along with their corresponding page numbers.

2. 🚲 **Cover Page** (1 point): Create an eye-catching cover page for your portfolio that includes an original title for your project as well as your name and the Classroom Presentation date.

3. 🚲 **Portfolio** (2 points): Organize all of your materials in a three-ring binder. The table of contents should come first, followed by your work from Portfolio Sections 1, 2, 3, and 4 above in the order presented. Your cover page should go on the front of the portfolio.

You have completed Component 1 of the Fitness Pursuit Project. By completing your portfolio, you have created an important resource that will help you work on Components 2 and 3. Though several worthy challenges lie ahead, you are now prepared to meet each of them, knowing that you have laid the necessary groundwork that will increase your chances for success. Good luck as you move on to creating your project exhibit items.

COMPONENT 2

CREATING YOUR FITNESS PURSUIT EXHIBIT

Total Possible Exhibit Points: 14 out of 100 total possible for project

Having thoroughly researched and organized your personal fitness information, it is now time to design and create an informative and appealing exhibit of your findings. The items you complete will be viewed by your classmates on the day of your Classroom Presentation and also by everyone who attends the Fitness Pursuit Expo at the end of the term. As always, put your best work into designing, creating, and integrating your exhibit items.

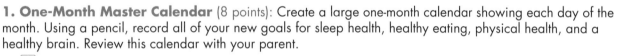

Note: Keep in mind that each item is only one part of the overall exhibit. In other words, no single item has to say everything about your project. Decide upon a purpose for each item. Consider how best to arrange your exhibit for the greatest effect.

1. One-Month Master Calendar (8 points): Create a large one-month calendar showing each day of the month. Using a pencil, record all of your new goals for sleep health, healthy eating, physical health, and a healthy brain. Review this calendar with your parent.

2. Display Board (3 points): Use a large two- or three-panel display board to create an "advertisement" for your Fitness Pursuit. It must include your one-month calendar, your project's title, and your name. You may then choose to add any of the required items or any additional materials that you wish.

3. Exhibit (3 points): Arrange your portfolio, sleep goal room art, and any additional materials you wish to include in an appealing and informative way.

You have now completed Component 2 of the Fitness Pursuit Project, an important exhibit that creatively displays your topic and findings. Now that you have finished your portfolio and exhibit, you are ready to confidently prepare for your Classroom Presentation (Component 3). Enjoy sharing your exciting project with your peers and teacher!

COMPONENT 3:

Giving Your Classroom Presentation
Total Possible Classroom Presentation Points: 5 out of 100 total possible for project

It is now time to share your personal fitness plans with others. Your Classroom Presentation is an opportunity to formally present some of your findings and to share some of your hard work. Relax and have fun with it.

1. 🚲 What to Include in Your Presentation:

- Sleep Goal Room Art (1 point): Share the art piece you designed for your room and explain how you decided upon your sleep goal.

- Personal Food Pyramid (1 point): Show your food pyramid. Tell the class which portions will be the most difficult for you to attain each day and explain how you plan to meet those goals.

- Safety Test (1 point): Ask the class an important question from your safety test and see if anyone can answer it correctly.

- Academic Activities List and Personalization (2 points): Explain one of your academic activities to the class. Share how you will personalize it for yourself.

> **Note:** Your Classroom Presentation should last three to four minutes and should be rehearsed, but not memorized. If you forget to include any required information, your teacher will ask you in a question form so that you have a chance to include it.

Bring to the Classroom Presentation:
All of your exhibit items and anything extra that you would like to enhance your exhibit.

You are now finished with Components 1, 2, and 3 - all of the assessed portions of your project. The final Component, Attending the Fitness Pursuit Expo, provides a festive closure to the Fitness Pursuit Project.

COMPONENT 4:

Attending the Fitness Pursuit Expo (The expo does not involve any points.)

Now that you have completed your project and presented it to your peers, it's time to share your work with family and friends at the Fitness Pursuit Expo. The expo is an event that recognizes and celebrates the hard work you have done on your Fitness Pursuit Project. At the expo, you will set up and stand by your exhibit as invited guests walk around informally and view the projects. Guests may ask you friendly questions about your project as they visit your exhibit, so have fun sharing your Fitness Pursuit findings with them.

Bring to the Expo: all of your exhibit items and anything extra that you would like to enhance your exhibit.

CONGRATULATIONS ON YOUR COMPLETED FITNESS PURSUIT PROJECT!

TEACHER FORMS CHECKLIST

use this checklist to record forms submitted by the students

student name	student commitment contract	student checkpoint organizer 1	student checkpoint organizer 2	student checkpoint organizer 3	expo invitation response number attending	special equip. needed
1.						
2.						
3.						
4.						
5.						
6.						
7.						
8.						
9.						
10.						
11.						
12.						
13.						
14.						
15.						
16.						
17.						
18.						
19.						
20.						
21.						
22.						
23.						
24.						
25.						

STUDENT COMMITMENT CONTRACT

expectations

project work time

I agree to:

- be responsible for following my Student Instruction Guide to do my work.
- keep track of all my project materials.
- work hard on Envision without disturbing others.
- save my unanswered questions until my teacher is free to talk.

checkpoint meetings

I will come prepared with:

- my Student Instruction Guide.
- my completed Student Checkpoint Organizer.
- all of my project materials.

important dates and times

Checkpoint 1: _____

Checkpoint 2: _____

Checkpoint 3: _____

Classroom Presentation: _____

Fitness Pursuit Expo: _____

_____

signatures

I agree to:

- meet expectations on the dates listed above.
- complete each of the Fitness Pursuit requirements to the best of my ability.
- bring my project work to school each day so that I can work on it during extra time.
- take my project work from school each night so that I can work on it at home.

I understand that the Envision Fitness Pursuit Project is a special opportunity, and that if I do not meet the above expectations, I may be asked to return to normal classroom activities.

Student Signature: _____ Date: _____

Parent Signature: _____ Date: _____

Please return this contract by: _____

STUDENT CHECKPOINT ORGANIZER

Student Name: _____ Checkpoint Date: _____

directions

1. Using your Student Instruction Guide, check off any requirements that you have completed up to this point.

2. Bring the following items to the Checkpoint Meeting:

• your Student Instruction Guide.

• your completed Student Checkpoint Organizer.

• all of your project materials.

questions

1. Which requirements have you completed up to this point?

_____

_____

2. Is there anything you need help with?

_____

_____

3. Is there anything else about your project that you would like to discuss?

_____

_____

4. List at least three goals you expect to accomplish by the next checkpoint.

_____

_____

TEACHER CHECKPOINT RECORD

student name	checkpoint 1 notes	checkpoint 2 notes	checkpoint 3 notes
1.			
2.			
3.			
4.			
5.			
6.			
7.			
8.			
9.			
10.			

FITNESS PURSUIT

YOU'RE INVITED!

EXPO INVITATION RESPONSE

Please fill out and return by: _____

Student Name: _____

Student Attending? ☐ Yes ☐ No

Number of Student Guests Attending: _____

Will your child need any special school equipment for the expo (i.e., computer or TV)? Please List: _____

_____

Thank you.

We look forward to seeing you at this special event!

FITNESS PURSUIT

PLEASE JOIN US FOR OUR ENVISION FITNESS PURSUIT EXPO!

Why? _____

Who? _____

Where? _____

When? _____

Remember to bring your camera!

FITNESS PURSUIT

CERTIFICATE OF ACHIEVEMENT

AWARDED TO

DATE

SIGNATURE

envision

FITNESS PURSUIT

166

FITNESS PURSUIT PROJECT

STUDENT

envision

fitness pursuit expo

envision®

TEACHER ASSESSMENT

Component 1: Building Your Project Portfolio
Total Possible Portfolio Points: 81 out of 100 total possible for project

Requirements	Possible Points	Teacher Points	Average Points
Portfolio Section 1: Sleep Health			
1. Sleep Log: For at least 14 days, keep a log of your sleep habits. Record your sleep amounts including any naps. Each evening before bed, reflect on and record how you felt throughout that day and give it a rating in your log. Include a key for your rating scale.	6		
2. Computer-Generated Double Line Graph: Using the computer, create a double line graph that shows every day you recorded in your sleep log, the hours of sleep you received for each, and your rating for each day. Include a graph title, a key, and your sleep log rating scale.	5		
3. Graph Analysis and Goal: Analyze your graph and below it write about any consistent patterns you notice. Using those observations, draw various conclusions about the ways different sleep patterns affect how you feel. Based on your conclusions, determine what you think is your personal optimal amount of daily sleep and state that as a goal. Discuss this with your parent.	5		
4. Sleep Goal Room Art: Create a piece of art that you can display in your bedroom. Your artwork should remind you of sleeping and should display your parent-approved sleep goal amount.	5		
Portfolio Section 2: Healthy Eating			
1. Healthy Eating Investigation: Investigate healthy eating recommendations for each main food group based on your gender, age, and size. Record recommended daily amounts for each group, and note specific food examples within each. Be sure that your sources are reliable and substantiated. Record your findings along with your information sources and analyze them for commonalities. Highlight the commonalities within each group.	5		
2. Personal Food Pyramid: Design and illustrate a detailed, daily food pyramid based on the commonalities you found in your healthy eating investigation. Be creative and make the pyramid attractive in contents and appearance. Share it with your parent.	5		
3. Healthy Eating Regimen: Using your personal food pyramid, plan one week's worth of optimal meals and snacks for yourself. You may organize it any way you wish. Take into account regular activities such as eating at school and participating in after-school activities. Review this plan with your parent who can help analyze it with respect to your personal health and lifestyle.	6		

TEACHER ASSESSMENT

Portfolio Section 3: Physical Health

1. Personal Exercise Guidelines: Examine exercise recommendations for your gender, age, and size including types of exercise and the duration of activity. Be sure that your sources are reliable and substantiated. Some source ideas are health care providers and governmental health agencies. Based on your findings, decide on general weekly personal guidelines for types of exercise and the durations of each activity. Explain your reasoning. Discuss this with your parent.	4		
2. Health Benefits Sentence Scramble: Investigate and record various health benefits of physical exercise. Read your information and choose what you think are the top ten benefits. Create a sentence scramble of ten sentences, each describing a benefit you chose. Include an answer key, write a title, and record directions for someone who might try your sentence scramble.	5		
3. Exercise Duration Clocks: Draw two non-digital clocks on a piece of paper. Label one "Weekdays" and label one "Weekends." On each clock, first draw the hands of the clock to show the time of day that you might begin an exercise activity. Next on each clock, shade the clock from your start time to the time you might stop the activity. Label the total duration times below each clock, making sure they correspond with your personal exercise guidelines. Lastly, write the name of a few activities you might choose to do during each exercise period. Share these with your parent.	5		
4. Safety Test: Create a test and answer key that assesses understanding of various age-appropriate safety issues. Some examples are bicycle and road safety, stranger safety, Internet safety, and safety in public places. Give the test to at least three peers and your parent. Correct the papers and review the results with each person.	5		

Portfolio Section 4: Healthy Brain

1. Academic Activity List: Make a list of academic activities that you would like to become better at or try for the first time. Your hobbies should be activities that help improve your academic knowledge base in various subject areas. Label each activity according to the ideal season in which you can participate in it. Reorganize your list so that you have two to three activities, listed in order of preference, in each seasonal subcategory.	6		
2. Academic Activity List Personalization: For each academic activity you listed, think of something specific and personally interesting that you can keep track of, and write it with its corresponding activity. For example, beside "Rock Collecting" you might write, "My List of Favorite Rocks" or for solving logic puzzles you might write, "Current Best Time in Seconds."	4		
3. Weekly Homework Schedule: Draw two non-digital clocks on a piece of paper. Label one "Weekdays" and label one "Weekends." On each clock, first draw the hands of the clock to show the time of day that you might begin an exercise activity. Next on each clock, shade the clock from your start time to the time you might stop the activity. Label the total duration times below each clock, making sure they correspond with your personal exercise guidelines. Lastly, write the name of a few activities you might choose to do during each exercise period. Share these with your parent.	5		

171

4. Stress and Calm Match-Up Illustration: To round out your total health plan, you will also consider stress in your life and how you might handle it. On the left side of a sheet of paper progressing downward, draw and label pictures of things that are stressful to you. On the right side of the paper, but not in the same order, draw and label pictures of something you can do to calm yourself in each situation. Draw a line from each stressful event to its appropriate calming solution to show your answers.	5		
Remaining Portfolio Materials			
1. Table of Contents: Write a table of contents that lists all the sections of your portfolio along with their corresponding page numbers.	2		
2. Cover Page: Create an eye-catching cover page for your portfolio that includes an original title for your project as well as your name and the Classroom Presentation date.	1		
3. Portfolio: Organize all of your materials in a three-ring binder. The table of contents should come first, followed by your work from Portfolio Sections 1, 2, 3, and 4 above in the order presented. Your cover page should go on the front of the portfolio.	2		
TOTAL PORTFOLIO POINTS	**81**		
Component 2: Creating Your Project Exhibit Total Possible Exhibit Points: 14 out of 100 total possible for project			
1. One-Month Master Calendar: Create a large one-month calendar showing each day of the month. Using a pencil, record all of your new goals for sleep health, healthy eating, physical health, and a healthy brain. Review this calendar with your parent.	8		
2. Display Board: Use a large two- or three-panel display board to create an "advertisement" for your Fitness Pursuit. It must include your one-month calendar, your project's title, and your name. You may then choose to add any of the required items or any additional materials that you wish.	3		
3. Exhibit: Arrange your portfolio, sleep goal room art, and any additional materials you wish to include in an appealing and informative way.	3		
TOTAL EXHIBIT POINTS	**14**		

Component 3: Giving Your Classroom Presentation
Total Possible Classroom Presentation Points: 5 out of 100 total possible for project

1. What to Include in Your Presentation:			
• Sleep Goal Room Art: Share the art piece you designed for your room and explain how you decided upon your sleep goal.	1		
• Personal Food Pyramid: Show your food pyramid. Tell the class which portions will be the most difficult for you to attain each day and explain how you plan to meet those goals.	1		
• Safety Test: Ask the class an important question from your safety test and see if anyone can answer it correctly.	1		
• Academic Activities List and Personalization: Explain one of your academic activities to the class. Share how you will personalize it for yourself.	2		
TOTAL CLASSROOM PRESENTATION POINTS	**5**		
TOTAL PROJECT POINTS	**100**		

STUDENT SELF-ASSESSMENT

Component 1: Building Your Project Portfolio
Total Possible Portfolio Points: 81 out of 100 total possible for project

Requirements	Possible Points	Student Points
Portfolio Section 1: Sleep Health		
1. Sleep Log: For at least 14 days, keep a log of your sleep habits. Record your sleep amounts including any naps. Each evening before bed, reflect on and record how you felt throughout that day and give it a rating in your log. Include a key for your rating scale.	6	
2. Computer-Generated Double Line Graph: Using the computer, create a double line graph that shows every day you recorded in your sleep log, the hours of sleep you received for each, and your rating for each day. Include a graph title, a key, and your sleep log rating scale.	5	
3. Graph Analysis and Goal: Analyze your graph and below it write about any consistent patterns you notice. Using those observations, draw various conclusions about the ways different sleep patterns affect how you feel. Based on your conclusions, determine what you think is your personal optimal amount of daily sleep and state that as a goal. Discuss this with your parent.	5	
4. Sleep Goal Room Art: Create a piece of art that you can display in your bedroom. Your artwork should remind you of sleeping and should display your parent-approved sleep goal amount.	5	
Portfolio Section 2: Healthy Eating		
1. Healthy Eating Investigation: Investigate healthy eating recommendations for each main food group based on your gender, age, and size. Record recommended daily amounts for each group, and note specific food examples within each. Be sure that your sources are reliable and substantiated. Record your findings along with your information sources and analyze them for commonalities. Highlight the commonalities within each group.	5	
2. Personal Food Pyramid: Design and illustrate a detailed, daily food pyramid based on the commonalities you found in your healthy eating investigation. Be creative and make the pyramid attractive in contents and appearance. Share it with your parent.	5	
3. Healthy Eating Regimen: Using your personal food pyramid, plan one week's worth of optimal meals and snacks for yourself. You may organize it any way you wish. Take into account regular activities such as eating at school and participating in after-school activities. Review this plan with your parent who can help analyze it with respect to your personal health and lifestyle.	6	

STUDENT SELF-ASSESSMENT

Portfolio Section 3: Physical Health

1. Personal Exercise Guidelines: Examine exercise recommendations for your gender, age, and size including types of exercise and the duration of activity. Be sure that your sources are reliable and substantiated. Some source ideas are health care providers and governmental health agencies. Based on your findings, decide on general weekly personal guidelines for types of exercise and the durations of each activity. Explain your reasoning. Discuss this with your parent.	4	
2. Health Benefits Sentence Scramble: Investigate and record various health benefits of physical exercise. Read your information and choose what you think are the top ten benefits. Create a sentence scramble of ten sentences, each describing a benefit you chose. Include an answer key, write a title, and record directions for someone who might try your sentence scramble.	5	
3. Exercise Duration Clocks: Draw two non-digital clocks on a piece of paper. Label one "Weekdays" and label one "Weekends." On each clock, first draw the hands of the clock to show the time of day that you might begin an exercise activity. Next on each clock, shade the clock from your start time to the time you might stop the activity. Label the total duration times below each clock, making sure they correspond with your personal exercise guidelines. Lastly, write the name of a few activities you might choose to do during each exercise period. Share these with your parent.	5	
4. Safety Test: Create a test and answer key that assesses understanding of various age-appropriate safety issues. Some examples are bicycle and road safety, stranger safety, Internet safety, and safety in public places. Give the test to at least three peers and your parent. Correct the papers and review the results with each person.	5	

Portfolio Section 4: Healthy Brain

1. Academic Activity List: Make a list of academic activities that you would like to become better at or try for the first time. Your hobbies should be activities that help improve your academic knowledge base in various subject areas. Label each activity according to the ideal season in which you can participate in it. Reorganize your list so that you have two to three activities, listed in order of preference, in each seasonal subcategory.	6	
2. Academic Activity List Personalization: For each academic activity you listed, think of something specific and personally interesting that you can keep track of, and write it with its corresponding activity. For example, beside "Rock Collecting" you might write, "My List of Favorite Rocks" or for solving logic puzzles you might write, "Current Best Time in Seconds."	4	
3. Weekly Homework Schedule: Create a schedule of a typical week and your main activities such as school, meals, sports, and other activities. Looking at each day's activities, set aside a daily block of time when you will do your homework. Take into consideration the typical amount of time your teachers and parents advise that you should be spending on homework each weekday and also on weekends.	5	

4. Stress and Calm Match-Up Illustration: To round out your total health plan, you will also consider stress in your life and how you might handle it. On the left side of a sheet of paper progressing downward, draw and label pictures of things that are stressful to you. On the right side of the paper, but not in the same order, draw and label pictures of something you can do to calm yourself in each situation. Draw a line from each stressful event to its appropriate calming solution to show your answers.	5	

Remaining Portfolio Materials

1. Table of Contents: Write a table of contents that lists all the sections of your portfolio along with their corresponding page numbers.	2	
2. Cover Page: Create an eye-catching cover page for your portfolio that includes an original title for your project as well as your name and the Classroom Presentation date.	1	
3. Portfolio: Organize all of your materials in a three-ring binder. The table of contents should come first, followed by your work from Portfolio Sections 1, 2, 3, and 4 above in the order presented. Your cover page should go on the front of the portfolio.	2	
TOTAL PORTFOLIO POINTS	**81**	

Component 2: Creating Your Project Exhibit
Total Possible Exhibit Points: 14 out of 100 total possible for project

1. One-Month Master Calendar: Create a large one-month calendar showing each day of the month. Using a pencil, record all of your new goals for sleep health, healthy eating, physical health, and a healthy brain. Review this calendar with your parent.	8	
2. Display Board: Use a large two- or three-panel display board to create an "advertisement" for your Fitness Pursuit. It must include your one-month calendar, your project's title, and your name. You may then choose to add any of the required items or any additional materials that you wish.	3	
3. Exhibit: Arrange your portfolio, sleep goal room art, and any additional materials you wish to include in an appealing and informative way.	3	
TOTAL EXHIBIT POINTS	**14**	

Component 3: Giving Your Classroom Presentation
Total Possible Classroom Presentation Points: 5 out of 100 total possible for project

1. What to Include in Your Presentation:		
• Sleep Goal Room Art: Share the art piece you designed for your room and explain how you decided upon your sleep goal.	1	
• Personal Food Pyramid: Show your food pyramid. Tell the class which portions will be the most difficult for you to attain each day and explain how you plan to meet those goals.	1	
• Safety Test: Ask the class an important question from your safety test and see if anyone can answer it correctly.	1	
• Academic Activities List and Personalization: Explain one of your academic activities to the class. Share how you will personalize it for yourself.	2	
TOTAL CLASSROOM PRESENTATION POINTS	**5**	
TOTAL PROJECT POINTS	**100**	

EXAMPLE
FITNESS PURSUIT
STUDENT RESOURCE CARDS

SLEEP LOG

A sleep log is a record of sleep patterns and other relevant sleep information recorded over a few weeks. It is helpful when trying to determine personal sleep patterns and useful for deciding whether or not your current sleep habits need any changes.

Create your log in a format that is most helpful to you. Try to define, "capture," and list a variety of time amounts: a lot of sleep, moderate sleep, and less sleep. Also try to "sleep in" a few times to see how long it takes your body to naturally wake up. Each evening before bed, reflect on and record how you felt throughout that day and give that day a rating such as "great," "good," or "bad" in your log. Create a key for your rating system.

EXAMPLE

EARL'S SLEEP LOG: WEEK ONE		
Day	**Hours of Sleep per Night**	**Next Day's Rating**
Saturday	10.5	4
Sunday	9	5
Monday	9	5
Tuesday	7	3
Wednesday	8	4
Thursday	7.5	4

Rating Scale Representing How I Felt the Next Day

5=Great
4=Good
3=Okay
2=Not Good
1=Bad
0=Terrible

COMPUTER-GENERATED DOUBLE LINE GRAPH

Double line graphs are an excellent way to display two sets of data that change over a period of time. Once the two sets of data are graphed, the graph can be used to determine possible relationships between the information.

To create your double line graph, start by recording each day from your sleep log along the bottom, or horizontal axis of the graph. On the vertical axis, up the left side of the graph, list numerical increments that will accommodate your sleep data and rating numbers. Next, record a dot for each hour amount above its corresponding day. Choose a color and connect the dots to form a colored line. Now, for each rating you chose, record a dot above its corresponding day. Choose a new color and connect those dots to form a differently colored line. Include a graph title, a key or legend, and your rating scale from your sleep log. This graph shows only a portion of a double line sleep graph.

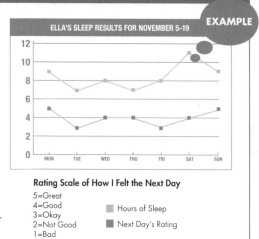

EXAMPLE

Rating Scale of How I Felt the Next Day

5=Great
4=Good
3=Okay
2=Not Good
1=Bad
0=Terrible

■ Hours of Sleep
■ Next Day's Rating

GRAPH ANALYSIS AND GOAL

The main purpose for creating a graph is to organize data in a way that is easy to visually analyze. Your double-line graph should help you see sleep habits that are beneficial to how you feel and those that are not.

To analyze your graph, look at each amount of sleep and how it corresponds to your rating for the next day. Suggestions for writing about your results are: Do you notice any consistent patterns? If so, what are they? From these patterns, what conclusions can you make about the amount of sleep you attain and how you feel the next day? Based on these results, what do you think is your personal optimal amount of nightly sleep?

EXAMPLE

Stephanie's Graph Analysis and Goal

After the nights that I attained nine hours of sleep, I usually felt great the next day. I noticed that on a couple of days following nights when I slept more than nine hours, I actually did not feel good. I also noticed that if I did not attain at least eight hours of sleep, I felt just okay at best the next day. Based on these results, it seems that I need at least eight hours of sleep every night to feel good. If I want to feel great, nine hours of sleep is best for me, so my nightly sleep goal will be nine hours.

PERSONAL FOOD PYRAMID

A food pyramid is one way to visualize the amounts and types of foods you should eat on a daily basis to maintain a healthy lifestyle. Although it is called a pyramid, your design can be drawn as a two-dimensional triangle if you like.

Your largest daily food group should be at the base of your pyramid. The remaining food groups should fill in the pyramid ascending in size from largest to smallest in order of each group's recommended amounts in your diet. Label each pyramid section according to its food group and illustrate various food examples within each. Your illustrated choices within each group should be based on your palate and lifestyle.

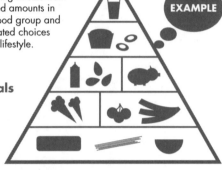

EXAMPLE

Alvina's Daily Healthy Food Goals

HEALTH BENEFITS SENTENCE SCRAMBLE

A sentence scramble is a puzzle that lists words from a sentence in an incorrect order. The person solving the puzzle must put the words in the correct order to discover the sentence and make sense out of it. Sentence scrambles are a fun way to become familiar with new ideas or terms. They also encourage people to rearrange and see things in new ways.

To create your sentence scramble, use a sheet of paper to write ten simple, separate sentences describing each health benefit you chose. On a second sheet of paper, in the same order as your list, record each sentence but with its words out of order. Double-check that each scrambled sentence contains all of its necessary words and no extra words. Write a title and directions for someone who might try your sentence scramble. Your original list of sentences can be your answer key.

Morgan's Animal Sentence Scramble

Directions: Unscramble each set of…

1. smell have keen a dogs of sense

2. like berries fish bears eat to and

3. have does lion female a mane a not

EXAMPLE

Animal Sentence Scramble Key

1. Dogs have a keen sense of smell.
2. Bears like to eat fish and berries.
3. A female lion does not have a mane.

EXERCISE DURATION CLOCKS

Being able to read the time of day on a clock is an important skill, especially when exercising. While exercising, it is important to keep your guidelines in mind so that you do not under- or over-exert yourself. Of course, for safety reasons, your exercise activities should always be monitored by a parent.

When drawing your exercise clocks, it is helpful to draw the numbers twelve and six first. Next, draw the numbers three and nine. From there, you can evenly space the numbers that fall between each. When you draw the hour hand, be sure to make it shorter than the minute hand. Remember to correctly label each set of clocks according to your Student Instruction Guide.

Weekdays 3:00 – 3:25
25 minutes total
Ride my bike…

EXAMPLE

Weekends 11:00 – 11:30
30 minutes total
Go swimming…

STRESS AND CALM MATCH-UP ILLUSTRATION

Match-up activities involve drawing a line to connect two items that go together in some way. Designing and solving these activities encourages creative thinking and knowledge assessment.

As you think of things that can be stressful to you, try to reflect on the past week or month. Recall events that were stressful to you and write them down. Are there certain types of events that were particularly stressful? If you have difficulty coming up with stressors you may want to ask parents, teachers, or friends for their opinions. Once you have a list of stressors, think of solutions you used, or could have used to calm yourself. Using these stressors and calming solutions, create your match-up illustration.

On the left side of a sheet of paper progressing downward, draw and label pictures of things that are stressful to you. On the right side of the paper, but not in the same order, draw and label pictures of something you can do to calm yourself in each situation. Draw a line from each stressful event to its appropriate calming solution to show your answers.

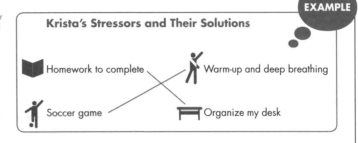

EXAMPLE

Krista's Stressors and Their Solutions

Homework to complete — Warm-up and deep breathing

Soccer game — Organize my desk

TABLE OF CONTENTS

Your table of contents should be the first page in your portfolio, although you write it after you finish all of the pages inside. Writing it after finishing the contents allows you to be accurate with your page numbers and titles in case you make any last-minute changes. Your table of contents should list each section and the page it begins on. It should be neat and well organized, but feel free to be creative with your own layout.

EXAMPLE

PORTFOLIO TABLE OF CONTENTS

Page Number	Section Title
1	Sleep Log
3	Computer-Generated Double Line Graph
4	Graph Analysis and Goal
5	Healthy Eating Investigation
8	Personal Food Pyramid

COVER PAGE

The cover page of your portfolio acts like the cover of a book. It should be eye-catching and should make someone want to open your portfolio to read about your topic and findings. It should include an original title for your project as well as your name and the Classroom Presentation date. Feel free to be creative and include artwork, design, and other creative touches.

FRONT COVER   SPINE   BACK COVER

EXAMPLE

LIVING HEALTHY, FEELING GREAT!

6·4·XX
BY TOM

FITNESS PURSUIT

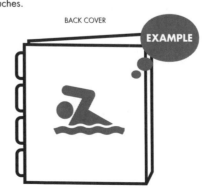

PORTFOLIO

Your portfolio is what you will use to organize most of your paper items. A standard one- to one-and-a-half-inch binder with a clear plastic overlay works well. Arrange the contents of the portfolio in the order that they are mentioned in your Student Instruction Guide. The cover should include your name, Classroom Presentation date, and an original project title. You may wish to add tab dividers for each section listed in your table of contents, clear page protectors for each piece of paper, and creative personal touches.

DISPLAY BOARD

The purpose of your display board is to draw attention to your project and to highlight some of its interesting information. It should be creative and colorful while remaining neat and well organized. Remember to make sure that it contains the necessary items listed on your Student Instruction Guide including your project's title and your name. The example below is to be used only as a guide; feel free to demonstrate your creativity. Tip: two- or three-panel corrugated display boards can be purchased at most craft stores. If you would rather make one, you can ask an adult to help construct one from a large cardboard box.

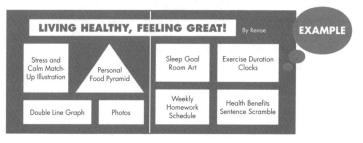

EXHIBIT

The purpose of your exhibit is to draw people's attention to your project. It should be neat, colorful, and creative. Your arrangement should include your exhibit items and any additional materials you wish to bring. The example below is to be used only as a guide; feel free to rearrange.

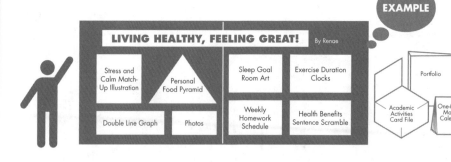

WHAT TO INCLUDE IN YOUR PRESENTATION

Your presentation will be a talk on what you learned, decided, and produced for your project. You should practice until you are comfortable with what you will say, but do not memorize a speech. Your presentation should be three to four minutes long and address the bulleted information listed in Component 3 your Student Instruction Guide. The additional suggestions below may help you prepare.

REMEMBER TO:

• Take a deep breath, relax, and enjoy sharing.

• Greet your audience and introduce yourself.

• Speak clearly, loudly enough so everyone can hear you, and at a natural pace.

• Stand still and calm; don't fidget.

• Point to and show various visuals as you speak about them.

• Have fun while presenting. Show your excitement about your experiences.

• Make eye contact with your audience, looking around the room naturally.

• Thank your audience when you are finished.

ABOUT THE AUTHOR

ABOUT THE AUTHOR

Melanie Bondy taught elementary students for several years before authoring the Envision program. She has always had a special interest in challenging students to reach their highest potential while making learning relevant and fun. When she saw a widespread need for higher quality materials for gifted students, she utilized her talents to create this unique educational program.

After publishing *Envision: Grade 5* just last year Melanie is thrilled to introduce the fourth grade Envision program to educators everywhere. The success of Envision has been overwhelming and its reviews have been purely positive. Melanie is now preparing to publish *Envision: Grade 3* followed by grades two, one, and six.

Melanie has also been a speaker at numerous gifted conferences nationwide, and has consulted with many school districts in several states. She is available and happy to discuss the presentation of the Envision program to teachers in your district.

Feel free to contact Melanie Bondy c/o:

Mind Vine Press

70727 Copper Boulevard

Lawton, MI 49065

Phone: 269.978.7227

Fax: 269.978.6871

Email: info@mindvinepress.com